Contents

"We Heard You . . . "

Dear Bass Pro Shops Customer:

The companies who thrive and are successful are those who listen to their customers. Thousands of you have expressed an interest in obtaining a directory of packages from hunting & fishing outfitters, guides and lodges; but you made it clear you wanted service providers who could be trusted to deliver an excellent value for your money.

It was from that desire this directory was born. Every outfitter, guide and lodge listed has been individually selected by our Bass Pro Shops Professional Hunting and Fishing Teams and writers, our Public Relations Department, and the Outdoor Wilderness Adventures staff.

The outfitters, guides and lodges listed in this directory are professionally operated and adhere to the Code of Ethics we have required them to sign. Our program to enlist your help in evaluating the performance of these businesses is designed to strengthen their adherence to that Code of Ethics. Unlike many other directories, none of the listings has been paid for by the outfitter, guide or lodge.

Many of the businesses listed are members of conservation groups such as Rocky Mountain Elk Foundation, Ducks Unlimited, the National Wild Turkey Federation, Quail Unlimited, and Trout Unlimited, and some are Orvis endorsed.

So please use the information in this Directory with confidence. Enjoy your wilderness adventure and rest assured: When you speak . . . we hear you.

Sincerely,
Bass Pro Shops

How This Directory Is Organized

This directory has been organized so it can be used easily. It is divided into four sections:

1. The first section consists of actual **Listings of Packages** by outfitters, guides and lodges with information as to how you may contact them directly to make a reservation. This section also indicates whether they offer Hunting (H), Fishing (F) or both Hunting & Fishing (H&F).
2. The second section consists of an **Alphabetical Index** of outfitters, guides and lodges listed in this directory.
3. The third section consists of a **Geographical Index** providing you with information regarding locations of outfitters, guides and lodges included in this directory.
4. At the end of the directory you will find an **Index to Species** which makes it convenient for you to find an outfitter, guide or lodge offering the type of hunting or fishing species in which you may be interested.

It is also divided into the following geographic areas:

- United States
- Canada
- Caribbean
- Central America and South America
- Other International Destinations

When reviewing the packages, please keep in mind that prices quoted are for land accommodations only (unless otherwise indicated) and *DO NOT* include air fare from your point of origin. Also, all accommodations and packages listed are subject to availability.

YOUR $18.95 REFUND

Remember, the $18.95 purchase price of this directory will be refunded to you from any outfitter, guide or lodge listed in this directory, when you book a trip with them. It will generally be credited toward your deposit check. (Value of your trip must be a minimum of $250.00.) When you make a reservation, be sure to let the outfitter, guide or lodge know, in advance, that you obtained their name from the *Bass Pro Shops' Hunting & Fishing Directory*. This will not only facilitate your receiving your $18.95 credit but will also assure you of receiving special VIP treatment.

HOW TO USE THE EVALUATION FORM

Inserted in this directory you will find a service provider Evaluation Form. After you visit any outfitter, guide or lodge listed in this directory, if you complete and mail in the form, you will receive by return mail a $10.00 Bass Pro Gift Certificate. The certificate is redeemable at any Bass Pro Shops Outdoor World Retail Store or when ordering through any Bass Pro Shops catalog. It is permissible to use photocopies of this form when multiple visits are involved.

DISCLAIMER OF LIABILITY

Outdoor Wilderness Adventures and Bass Pro Shops and their affiliates are providing information regarding services offered by outfitters, guides and lodges and assumes no liability for any loss, expense, damage, accident, delay, inconvenience, injury or weather which results, directly or indirectly, from any act or failure to act, whether negligent or otherwise, of any outfitter, guide or lodge listed in this directory of packages. Outdoor Wilderness Adventures and Bass Pro Shops further make no guarantees that may result from such hunting and/or fishing or the effect of poor weather conditions.

We know things change. To get up-to-the-minute information on the standing of outfitters, guides and lodges in this directory or check for recent additions to the listings which will appear in revised editions, visit http://guides.basspro.com.

Code of Ethics

FOR YOUR PROTECTION AND SATISFACTION, EVERY OUTFITTER, GUIDE AND LODGE IN THIS DIRECTORY HAS SIGNED THIS CODE OF ETHICS

I, the undersigned, hereby agree to the following:

I agree to be fully insured and bonded and promise to adhere to the Federal, State and local regulations that apply to my profession.

I agree to utilize my experience and skills to satisfy my clients, and commit myself to consistently perform my job in an excellent manner.

I agree to continuously service the equipment I use so that it will always be in excellent condition. This includes boats, motors, tents and other equipment required in servicing my clients.

I agree to market my services to potential clients in a professional manner and will not mislead them regarding the services I offer or the cost of those services.

I agree to service my clients with the highest quality food and facilities available in harmony with the local environment and culture.

I agree to do my best to preserve the delicate balance between wildlife, habitat and humans.

I commit myself to the preservation of the world's fish and game species so that the joys and wonders of a wilderness adventure can be experience by children for generations to come.

Outfitters, Guides & Lodges

(H) HUNTING, (F) FISHING, (H&F) HUNTING & FISHING

UNITED STATES

ALABAMA

BARTON RIDGE PLANTATION (H&F)
Rockford, Alabama
Quail/Turkey

Over 5000 acres intensely managed for wildlife. Quail hunt from Oct.–Feb. We offer terrain to suit every hunter. Guided & self-hunts available. Turkey hunts Mar.–Apr. with the most professional turkey callers in the country. Comfortable lodge accommodations with home-style cooking. Open year round for hiking, canoeing, fishing, floating Hatchet Creek or just getting back to nature. For more information or Video, call 800-953-7330.

STEELWOOD (H&F)
Loxley, Alabama
Bass/Quail/Pheasant

For a truly unique outdoor experience, escape to Steelwood, where nature's simplicity combines with elegant resort community sophistication. Steelwood is known for its relaxed pace, dedication to quality and personal attention to detail. Our lodges feature 12 bedrooms, each with its own private bath. Each lodge overlooks beautiful 200-acre Steelwood Lake and Alabama's #2 ranked golf course *(Golf Digest)*. After a day of bass fishing and quail or pheasant hunting, relax on the Clubhouse porch by the outdoor fireplace and watch the sun set on the tranquil lake's waters. A gourmet meal awaits you inside the Clubhouse or casual dining can be enjoyed back at your lodge. Just 25 miles to the south is the Gulf of Mexico, where saltwater fishing is available year-round. In addition to deluxe accommodations and outdoor recreational activities, Steelwood offers exceptional meeting facilities. Packages begin at $275 per day, per person, double occupancy (includes lodging, all meals, half-day fishing trip, golf and more). Limited offer. Pheasant and Quail hunting extra.

Phone: 800-264-2297

ALASKA

AFOGNAK WILDERNESS LODGE (H&F)
Seal Bay, Alaska
Kodiak Brown Bear/Roosevelt Elk/Sitka Blacktail Deer/Sea Ducks/ Salmon/Halibut/Trout/Ling Cod/ Sea Bass/Red Snapper

Spring and Fall hunting, Spring through Fall fresh and saltwater fishing, and up-close wildlife photography in and around Afognak Island State Park of Kodiak area. Elegant log lodge in the heart of true wilderness, superb local cuisine, floatplane access, experienced guides, international references, excellent reputation since 1974 with both sportsmen and families.

Phone: 800-478-6442
Fax: 907-486-2217
huntafognak@usa.net
www.afognaklodge.com
www.huntafognak.com

ALAGNAK LODGE (F)
Bristol Bay Region, Alaska
Salmon/Rainbow Trout

The Alagnak Lodge sits atop a bluff overlooking the wild and scenic Alagnak River in the heart of Alaska's premier wilderness fishing area, the Bristol Bay watershed. Fish for all five species of Pacific salmon, chrome bright in the tidal water in front of the lodge. Upriver and optional flyouts take us to Alaska's famous trophy rainbow trout, graying and char. Comfortable accommodations, excellent food, and a friendly atmosphere will greet you in the lodge at the end of your day on the river.

Phone: 800-877-9903
tony@alagnaklodge.com
www.alagnaklodge.com

ALASKAN ADVENTURES (H)
Port Alsworth, Alaska
Moose/Grizzly Bear/Black Bear/ Caribou/Wolves/Brown Bear/Sheep

Registered Alaska Hunting Guide Rocky McElveen can make you one of the few fortunate ones able to reach the remote areas that are home to moose, caribou, black bear, brown bear, grizzly bear, Dall sheep and Alaskan timber wolf. Using high-powered Super Cub planes with tundra tires or floats, we are able to track and position the select few who truly want Alaska trophy hunting. Our spike camps are carefully scouted and selected to produce quality hunts. 5600 Foothill Road, Rocklin, CA 95677.

Phone: 800-392-6210.
www.alaskan-adventures.com

ALASKAN DROP HUNTS WITH ALLGOOD FLYING SERVICE (H)
Chugiak, Alaska
Moose/Caribou/Black Bear

Hunting season begins the first day of August and runs into October. Now is the time to call and reserve your hunt for moose, caribou, black bear or any combination of all hunts. You'll be transported in a Piper Super Cub 180, piloted by owner/operator Ken Alligood. I have lived in Alaska for thirty years and have over 7000 hours of bush flying. The Super Cub is the workhorse of Alaska, making it challenging for remote areas. All clients are checked on during their hunt every other day, weather permitting, insuring a safe and more successful hunt. Guided and unguided hunts available. So get on board and book your hunt for Alaska today!

Phone: 907-694-1886
www.allgoodflying.com

ALASKAN FISHING ADVENTURES (F)
Alaska's Kenai Peninsula
Saltwater, Freshwater,
Flyfishing/Wildlife Tours/Whale-
Watching/Kenai Fjord & Glacier
Tours/Shopping Tours

Discover unequaled fishing and lodging choices in Alaska's playground, the Kenai Peninsula. Choose between our different lodges, we have one that is right for you. Ocean front, river front or secluded condominiums in the forest, we have the perfect accommodations. Enjoy daily fishing on Cook Inlet for king salmon and halibut, the Kenai River for king salmon and silver salmon, drift boat trips on the Kasilof River, trophy rainbow trout charters, fly-in trips and multiple species trips on the scenic Resurrection Bay in Seward. Specializing in one-day outings or multiple-day lodging-fishing packages. Charters include

all gear and tackle and fish processing. Serving anglers worldwide since 1976. Offering unbeatable air fares to Alaska and discounted car rental rates. All inclusive packages from: 3 days/4 nights $2195 pp/dbl occp.; 7 nights/6 days $3195 pp/dbl occp.

Phone: 800-548-3474
Tim@alaskanfishing.com
www.alaskanfishing.com

ALASKA'S TROPHY KING LODGE (F)
Kenai Peninsula, Alaska
King & Silver Salmon/Halibut/
Rainbow Trout

We offer the only full-service, 4-star operation on the Kenai Peninsula for combination saltwater and stream fishing. We fish May–Aug. in the Cook Inlet and the Kenai and Kasilof Rivers (spin-cast or fly fishing). Gourmet meals, daily maid service, top-shelf liquor, professional guides and incredible fishing. Featured in *Sport Fishing* magazine as an "Alaska Hot Spot." 5- and 7-day all-inclusive packages from $2800 per person.

Phone: 800-972-4320
www.trophyking.com

ALASKA'S VALHALLA LODGE (H&F)
Iliamna-Katmai-Bristol Bay, Alaska
Rainbow Trout/Pacific Salmon/
Ptarmigan

Secluded in the wilderness heartland of Alaska's finest fishing is a premier lodge offering you the highest quality Alaska experience. Daily floatplane fly-outs, jet boats and rafting put you on top-producing streams in the Iliamna-Katmai-Bristol Bay sportfisheries; rainbow trout, lake trout, dolly varden trout, arctic grayling, northern pike, and five species of Pacific salmon. Explore and fish uncrowded streams and relax in secure comfort at Valhalla Lodge. Limited to 10 anglers per week. Orvis-endorsed lodge. One-week packages from $4500.00 per person per week, double occupancy.

Phone: 907-243-6096
Fax: 907-243-6095
www.valhallalodge.com

ANGLER'S CHOICE LODGE (F)
Port Althorp, Alaska
King/Silver/Pink/Chum/Pacific Halibut/Ling Cod

The choice of the serious fisherman. Guests can enjoy weekend, midweek and full-week saltwater fishing packages at Angler's Choice Lodge. Located 40 minutes by seaplane from Juneau, near the entrance to beautiful Glacier Bay National Park, the lodge is in the heart of prime sportfishing grounds. This means less time spent traveling to and from the fabulous fishing grounds, and more time spent fishing for king, silver, pink, and chum salmon, Pacific halibut, and ling cod. From experienced boat captains and big fish, to beautiful scenery, fine food and real Alaskan hospitality, Angler's Choice Lodge offers you a world-class saltwater fishing experience.

Phone: 800-858-5591
Fax: 907-789-1749
aksportfsh@aol.com
www.anglerschoicelodge.com

BARANOF EXPEDITIONS (H&F)
Cape Ommaney Lodge, Southeast Alaska
Brown Bear/Black Bear/Sitka Deer/ Mountain Goat/Salmon/Steelhead/ Halibut/Trout

We provide professional, first-class trophy hunting and fishing to a limited number of clients. Spring and Fall hunting. Boat and lodge-based 8- to 10-day packages from $5000 to $12,500 per person. Spectacular summer fishing, 4 full days of fresh and saltwater fishing for Wild Alaskan King Salmon, Silver Salmon, Halibut and Trout. Packages available for $2795 per person. Our lodge is located 65 miles south of Sitka on the southern tip of Baranof Island.

Phone: 907-747-3934
Fax: 907-747-5911
boyce@ptialaska.net
www.baranofexpeditions.com

BEARFOOT ALASKA RESORT & LODGE (F)
Dillingham, Alaska
King/Rainbow/Sockeye/Silver/Dolly Varden/Arctic Char/Arctic Grayling/ Northern Pike

Fishing the world-famous Alaska Bristol Bay. Eleven species of native wild fish, no hatchery fish here. Fabulous Fly Fishing for the novice to expert. All trips are guided and each guest receives a complimentary day of fly-out fishing to a remote stream. A full-service lodge with great cuisine and fully furnished guest rooms with private baths. Daily fly-outs. Packages starting at $2495. Cooperate incentive programs available.

Phone: 888-684-0177
bearfootak@aol.com
www.bearfootalaska.com

BOARDWALK WILDERNESS LODGE (F)
Prince of Wales Island, Alaska
Guided Fresh & Saltwater Fishing

The Boardwalk Lodge is small and relaxed, a place where guests experience some of the finest steelhead, salmon, cutthroat, and Dolly Varden fishing in southeastern Alaska. Located on Prince of Wales Island—43 miles northwest of Ketchikan, two hours by plane from Seattle—the lodge is near the confluence of the Thorne River and Thorne Bay. Because of our proximity to fresh and salt water, anglers can also "test the deep" for halibut, ling cod, red snapper, and salmon aboard heated cabin cruisers. Non-fishing activities are also available. After a day of fishing, relax in the outdoor hot tub and snack on hors d'oeuvres as you sip cabernet sauvignon and watch eagles, deer and black bear forage across the tidal inlet. Dinner is a gourmet delight! Our chef prepares local dishes with a flair unsurpassed anywhere in the state. Open May through September.

Phone: 800-764-3918
Fax: 907-828-3367
www.boardwalklodge.com

BRISTOL BAY LODGE (F)
Dillingham, Alaska
Rainbow Trout/Arctic Char/Arctic Grayling/Northern Pike/LakeTrout/Dolly Varden/ Salmon—5 Species

The fishing experience of a lifetime in the grand Alaskan tradition. Bristol Bay Lodge. Since 1972, one of Alaska's premier wilderness fishing lodges providing anglers from around the world the opportunity for the finest the "Great Land" has to offer. Located in the Wood-Tikchik-Togiak region. Flyout to remote rivers. Ron or Maggie McMillan.

Phone: 509-964-2094
Fax: 509-964-2269

BRISTOL BAY SPORTFISHING/ ILIAMNA LAKE LODGE (F)
Iliamna, Alaska
Trophy Rainbow/Silvers/Kings/Char/Dolly Varden

One of the oldest and most respected fly-out lodges in Alaska. Located on Lake Iliamna and centered in the middle of the finest freshwater fisheries in the world. Trophy rainbow, silvers, kings, char, Dolly Varden and seven other species of game fish. We pride ourselves in offering the most diverse fishing, sightseeing and wildlife experience available. Gourmet Alaska-style meals, shore lunches, fly-outs, jet boats, fishing gear and personalized service from arrival to departure are all inclusive. June-Sept., 5-night packages: $3850. 7-night packages: $4850.

Winter: 907-571-1325
Summer: 208-255-2694
www.bristol-bay.com

DON DUNCAN'S ALASKA PRIVATE GUIDE SERVICE (H&F)
Nushagak River, Alaska
Grayling/Dollies/Pike/Char/King Salmon/Red/Silver/Brown Bear/Moose/Caribou

Fishing for king, red, and silver salmon in a trophy rainbow area with grayling, dollies, pike and char. July–Sept. Weekly rates for 1x4 $1400; 1x2 $2000; 1x1 $2700. Spring Brown Bear and Fall Moose and Caribou hunts with high success rates and excellent fishing. Excellent riverside and fly-in camp accommodations. Fully guided, semi-guided, outfitter unguided, or drop-off hunts available. Great photo opportunities. 299 Alvin St., Fairbanks, AK 99712. Member N.R.A. & Charter Member N.A.F.C.

Phone: 907-457-8318
apgs@rica.net
www.apgs.com

FISH ON! WITH GARY KERNAN (F)
Kenai, Alaska
King/Red/Silver/Pink/Trophy Trout/ Halibut

Fishing 5 different rivers, including the Kenai, world famous for trophy Kings exceeding 80 lbs. running mid-May through July, 750,000 Reds in June and July, and thousands of Silvers in August and September. These rivers are a fly-fisherman's paradise. Halibut fishing May through September ranging 20 to 400 lbs. Three-day king salmon guided fishing package, including 4 nights lodging, with 3 half-days fishing (5-6 hrs. each day) $913. Enhanced packages including bear viewing, glacier cruises and fly-out fishing. Group rates also available.

Toll Free: 888-283-4002
bigfish@alaska.com
www.alaskafishon.com

FOREST-VIEW LODGE & CONDOS (F)
Soldotna, Alaska
King Salmon/Giant Halibut/Huge Ling Cod/Trophy Rainbow Trout/ Coho Salmon

Affordable modern two- and three-bedroom condominiums offer outstanding value set in the midst of the world's best saltwater and freshwater king salmon and halibut fishing. Featuring tastefully furnished units, full kitchen, tub/shower bathrooms, extra long twin or king beds and televisions. You can choose to prepare your own meals (groceries can be purchased nearby) or dine at one of the many restaurants in the area. Daily maid service, on-site laundry, and barbecue area are included. Daily guided fishing charters include salmon, halibut, trout, ling cod and rockfish. This is the perfect location for families, groups or couples who prefer to do things "their own way." A la carte nightly lodging rates from $175-$295 per night. 4 night/3 day lodging/fishing package $1395 pp/dbl occp.

Phone: 800-548-3474
timmyberg@yahoo.com
www.alaskanfishing.com

4 W AIR (H&F)
Soldotna, Alaska
Salmon/Trout/Grayling/Pike/Char/ Caribou/Moose/Black Bear/Wolf/ Wolverine/Ptarmigan/Grouse

A licensed/insured air taxi providing hunters reasonably priced unguided hunts since 1984. Operating a DeHavilland Beaver on floats, Bill does all the flying. Mulchatna caribou herd hunts begin at $1318.75 per person. We also provide a wall tent-based fishing camp located in the heart of the Bristol Bay/Iliamna fishery. World-class fishing from our comfortable camp is $2800 per person, includes 6 nights, 7 days, with 5 full days of fully guided flyout fishing. Plane and pilot stay with you always.

Phone: 907-776-5370 (voice & fax)
fourwair@alaska.net
www.alaska.net/~fourwair

GLACIER BAY'S BEAR TRACK INN (F)
Gustavus, Alaska
Fresh/Saltwater Fishing and Glacier Tours/Dolly Varden Trout/Cutthroat/ Steelhead/Pink Salmon/Silver/ Chum/Sockeye

This remarkable luxury inn must be seen to be believed. Offering complete packages which include world-class fishing, kayaking, whale watching, glacier tours, wildlife and more. You can fish for Dolly Varden, cutthroats, steelheads, pink salmon, silvers, chums and sockeye. 5Days/5Nights $2767 per person. Includes round-trip air fare from Juneau, lodging meals, boat, tackle, guide, licenses and fish packaging.

Call toll free: 888-697-2284.
beartrac@aol.com
www.beartrackinn.com

GOODNEWS RIVER LODGE (F)
Anchorage, Alaska
King/Silver/Chum/Pink/Sockeye Salmon/Rainbow Trout/Grayling/Char

The Goodnews River Lodge is located on a pristine western Alaska river that empties into the Bering Sea. Enjoy fishing for all 5 species of Pacific salmon, rainbow trout, Arctic grayling, and char within minutes of the lodge. You stay in comfortable, heated 2-person tent-cabins. We are the only lodge on the river, and we feature a 2:1 guest to guide ratio with top-of-the-line equipment to maximize our chances of hooking the big one! That's why ESPN's "Fly Fishing the World" rates us #1 among the top 100 fisheries in the world.

Phone: 800-274-8371
grlcamp@bellsouth.net
www.epicfishing.com

GREAT ALASKA ADVENTURE LODGE (F)
Kenai Peninsula, Alaska
Seven-Day Natural History Safari with 1 Bear Viewing Overnight

Alaska's finest adventure travel itinerary. Seven days of adventure: Denali flightseeing, private brown bear viewing, river rafting, hiking, remote camps, fishing, optional biking, canoeing and kayaking. Active and relaxed versions available. Small groups with personal touches, 3-star lodge, fantastic meals and award-winning remote camps. Nightly happy hour, fishing and paddling. Nineteen years at same incredible location. 7D/6N: $2395 to $3795.

Phone: 800-544-2261 (ask for Kent or Laurence John)
greatalaska@greatalaska.com

GREAT ALASKA FISH CAMP (F)
Kenai Peninsula, Alaska
Halibut/King/Red/Silver/Pink/Trout/ Char

The Kenai Peninsula offers some of the most spectacular scenery and sportfishing in America. Our lodge and fly-in remote camps serve up incredible variety—the world's largest king salmon and halibut, along with bountiful runs of sockeye, coho and pink salmon. World-class rainbow trout and char (spin or fly) plus a day trip to our remote bear viewing camp in Lake Clark National Park round out a memorable week. Three-star accommodations, nightly happy hour and dynamite shore fishing in front of lodge. 7D/6N Package: $2395 to $3795 from Kenai.

Phone: 800-544-2261 (ask for Kent or Laurence John)
greatalaska@greatalaska.com

HOLITNA RIVER LODGE (F)
Holitna River, Alaska
King Salmon/Silvers/Chum/Northern Pike/Sheefish/Char/Grayling

Experience the Holitna Retreat! A week in the Alaskan Bush. This is the remote Alaskan Wilderness Adventure. The Holitna River Lodge is located on a remote Alaskan River with the nearest village, Sleetemute, 46 miles away. Hunt the way the natives hunt! Fish in waters where the fish have never seen a lure! Challenge yourself to guided or unguided hunting (bow/rifle) or fishing excursions at rates that make sense. This lodge is perfect for the capable outdoorsman! Cabins, boats, motors and fresh garden included in packages.

Phone: 800-392-6210
www.alaskan-adventures.com

INLET VIEW LODGE (F)
Kenai, Alaska
Luxury Lodging and Legendary Fishing. Halibut/Salmon/Trout/Ling Cod/Wildlife Viewing/Fly-Ins

Exclusive beachside setting offers spectacular vistas of Cook Inlet and the distant towering volcanoes of the Alaska Range. With exquisite rooms, outdoor hot tub, volleyball court, spacious decks, romantic sunsets and excellent cuisine, this sensational property offers a unique blend of Alaska. Humpback whales, orcas, brown bears, otters, moose, caribou, eagles and more during your stay. Daily guided fishing for the world's largest king salmon, coho salmon, sockeye salmon, trout, char, ling cod, halibut and more. Everything included: guides, boats, tackle, baits, meals, fish processing. Spacious but intimate, we can accommodate only 12 guests. The Inlet View Lodge is the perfect choice for any Alaskan fishing getaway. 4D/3N $1895 pp, dbl occp; 7N/6D $2795 pp, dbl occp.

Phone: 800-548-3474
timmyberg@yahoo.com
www.alaskanfishing.com

KATMAI LODGE (F)
Bristol Bay, Alaska
King Salmon/Sockeye/Chum/Pink/ Silver/Rainbow Trout/Grayling/ Char/Dolly Varden/Northern Pike

Come and enjoy the magic of Alaska from the comfort of Katmai Lodge on the banks of the Alagnak River, 300 miles from the nearest road. Fish for five species of Salmon, Rainbow Trout, Grayling, Char, Dolly Varden and Northern Pike. We are located in the only designated Trophy fishing area in Alaska. We offer single, double or triple rooms with a private bath: 3 nights—$2800. 4 nights—$3500. 7 nights—$5000. Come and go on your own schedule. We offer special group packages and rates.

Phone: 800-330-0326
Katmai@Katmai.com
www.Katmai.com

KENAI RIVERBEND RESORT (F)
Kenai Peninsula, Alaska
Trophy Salmon and Halibut Fishing

Enjoy legendary Alaskan fresh and saltwater sportfishing along with the finest log cabins and lodge on the Kenai! Experience rod-bending, line-stripping action for the world's largest king salmon, acrobatic silver salmon, monster halibut, knuckle-busting sockeye salmon, trophy native rainbows, and huge ling cod and rockfish. We offer you Alaska's best guides for great fishing adventure along with tournament-grade rods and reels, luxury riverfront lodging and service you deserve! Join us this summer for some of the best fishing Alaska has to offer!

Phone: 800-625-2324
www.kenairiverbend.com

KNIKTUK OUTFITTERS (H&F)
Dillingham, Alaska
Brown Bear/Grizzly Bear/Black Bear/ Alaska Yukon Moose/Barren Ground Caribou/Wolf/Wolverine

Offering Spring and Fall hunts in southwest Alaska. Play your hunt to your pocket book. We offer hunts, fully guided, from $3500 to $3950.

Great success rate and reasonably priced Brown Bear hunts. Complimentary fishing for salmon and trout. New lodge built in 2000.

Phone: 888-684-0177
renew1@aol.com
www.kniktuk.com

LAKE CLARK LODGE (F)
Port Alsworth, Alaska
Grayling/Arctic Char/Rainbow Trout/ Northern Pike/Sockeye Salmon

Lake Clark Lodge is located on Lake Clark, the headquarters of Lake Clark National Park. This is the ultimate 6-day flyout fishing trip! It includes room and board at our first-class Alaskan Lodge with full use of our facility. You will flyout at least 3 of these days for remote wilderness fishing. Most weeks will include a fish and float or a special jet boat trip on selected rivers. All freezing and packaging of your first 40 lbs. of fish included. Contact us for package prices.

Phone: 800-392-6210
www.alaskan-adventures.com

LARRY RIVERS MASTER GUIDE & OUTFITTER (H)
Talkeetna, Alaska
Alaskan Grizzly Bear

Grizzly hunting like most hunters only dream about. Seeing 5 or 6 grizzly and a dozen black bear a day is common. Most clients take both. All access is by Supercub to tundra airstrips in the mountains behind the lodge. You won't see roads, hunters or day-glo orange. That's Alaska! 10-day fall grizzly hunt (1x1) $8850. Includes all camp gear and spike camp. Everything the hunter is going to need for the hunt other than license and big game tag.

Phone: 800-393-2471
larry@larryrivers.com
www.larryrivers.com

MIKE CUSACK'S KING SALMON LODGE (F)
King Salmon, Alaska
Salmon/Trout/Grayling/Char/Pike

We provide everything, from top-of-the-line fishing gear to world-class cuisine, in an effort to ensure your enjoyment. World-class rainbow trout, Dolly Varden, grayling, Arctic char, northern pike, and five species of salmon abound in Bristol Bay's fertile waters. When not fishing, take advantage of flight-seeing or wildlife viewing opportunities. No incidentals bill. 7D/7N Package: $6500 or $1000/day.

Phone: 800-437-2464
Fax: 907-563-7929

NORTHWOODS LODGE (F)
Lake Creek, Alaska
Freshwater Salmon/Rainbow Trout/ Grayling/Northern Pike/Whitefish/ Ling Cod

Your Alaskan fishing adventure begins at Lake Hood Float Plane Base in Anchorage where you will fly 65 air miles northwest to Northwoods Lodge. The 45-minute flight will take you over some of Alaska's most productive salmon streams. The lodge is located on the banks of Fish Lakes Creek, one of the many clear water tributaries of the Yentna River. Our streams are bursting with huge returns of kings, silvers and sockeye, as well as chum and pink salmon, rainbow trout, Arctic grayling and northern pike. Guest accommodations are well-appointed double-occupancy cabins overlooking Fish Lakes Creek. The main lodge is the gathering place for gourmet meals and relaxing after a hard day of fishing. All trips are fully guided and outfitted.

Phone: 800-999-6539
www.northwoodslodge.net

OUZEL EXPEDITIONS (F)
Alaska and Russia
Rainbows/Salmon/Char/Grayling

Ouzel prides itself as the highest quality fly-in raft trip company in Alaska and Russia. We provide fishing and wilderness vacation experiences for 6-9 days. Trips are outfitted with top-notch guides and the best equipment. Fresh delicious meals are prepared by your expert guides. Paul and Sharon started Ouzel in 1978. Areas are: Bristol Bay, Western Alaska, Alaska Peninsula, Upper Cook Inlet and the Brooks Range, including Arctic National Wildlife Refuge, and Kamchatka, Russia. Prices range from $2800 to $4000.

Phone: 800-825-8196
Fax: 907-783-3220
paul@ouzel.com
www.ouzel.com

PARKER GUIDE SERVICE (H)
Southeast Alaska
Black Bear/Brown Bear/ Mountain Goat

First-class yacht-based hunts for Spring/Fall black bear, brown bear and late season mountain goat. Hunt National Forest Service land under special use permit. No drawings, just license and tag fees. Top-notch personal service, gourmet meals, and a warm bed. No ocean swells. We anchor in secluded calm waters. 10-Day brown bear hunt 1x1, 5-day black bear 2x1, and 7-day 2x1 goat hunts 95%–100% success rate.

Toll Free: 877-654-HUNT
akguide@ptialaska.net
www.ptialaska.net/~akguide

PYBUS POINT LODGE (H&F)
Admiralty Island National Monument, Alaska
Halibut/Salmon/Trout/Black Bear/Brown Bear/Blacktail Deer/Ducks/Geese

Fly into some of the finest freshwater and fly fishing in Alaska on world-famous Admiralty Island. Large main log lodge. Private cabins overlooking snow-capped mountains. Hot tub and sauna. Giant halibut, all species of salmon, trout, steelhead. Remote fly out. Largest concentration of brown bears and humpback whales and bald eagles in the world, black bears and blacktail deer. Gourmet meals. For both the hunter and fisherman. Photography. Licensed Coast Guard skippers and boats. Fish packing. We host only 20 guests. Fishing: May and June; 5 Day/5 Night Package: $2395. Hunting: Sept. 5D/5N black bear & deer: $4000, single, guided.

Phone: 800-94-PYBUS
www.pybus.com

RAINBOW TROUT NET (F)
Dillingham, Alaska
Arctic Char/Grayling/Rainbow Trout/ Dolly Varden/Silver Salmon/King Salmon/Sockeye Salmon

A fisherman's paradise located on Alaska's longest freshwater river. Whether you fly fish or spin fish, are a novice or an expert, our experienced guides will show you the honey holes of this fabulous river located in the world-renowned Bristol Bay. Your stay will be in heated wilderness tent cabins located on the river's shoreline. Hot water showers and home cooking will make your trip a lifetime remembrance. Five-day packages available that include floatplane from Dillingham, AK. Limited to six guests per week.

wildstream@aol.com
www.rainbowtrout.net

ROD & GUN RESOURCES/ ALASKA WILDERNESS SAFARI (F)
Alaska
Salmon/Arctic Char/Dolly Varden

Rod & Gun Resources' Alaska Wilderness Safari, southwest of King Salmon, Alaska, offers spectacular mixed-bag fishing for sea-bright pink, chum and silver salmon, arctic char and dolly varden—in the midst of breathtaking scenery, with high-tech comfort. The program includes two days of helicopter fly-out fishing in a meticulously maintained Bell Ranger helicopter. This enables us to fish never-before-fished waters and gives you a bird's-eye view of the magnificent peninsula scenery. 7 night/7 day fishing package is $3995, which includes two day helicopter fly-out. Air travel and tips not included.

Phone: 800-211-4753

www.rodgunresources.com

SEE ALASKA WITH JIM H. KEELINE (H&F)
Yakutat, Alaska
Silver Salmon/Dolly Varden/Coho/ King/Brown Bear/Black Bear/Moose Mountain Goat/Wolf/Ducks/Geese

We hunt black and brown bear in Spring starting late April and ending late March. All brown bear hunts are 10 days. This does not count your day in or out of camp. You get 10 days to hunt. When you book a 7-day black bear hunt, you get 5 days of hunting. All fishing trips are 5 days. They start the day you arrive. We have great silver salmon fishing in late August to mid-September. Hunting in fall starts late August and runs until mid-October. You can hunt single or multi-species: moose, brown bear, mountain goat and black bear. All hunts are 10 days as in the Spring.

Phone: 907-784-3711 (in season)
Winter: 712-336-5124
Fax: 712-336-0923
keeline@ncn.net

SILVER SALMON CREEK LODGE (F)
Soldotna, Alaska
Silver Salmon/Halibut/Char/ Rainbows

A full-service fly-in lodge on Cook Inlet approaching its 20th season under the same management. We specialize in adventurous opportunities for ocean-fresh silver salmon, Dolly Varden, char, sea-bright chum salmon, and off shore halibut. With renowned food service and a maximum guest load of 12, we strive for quality experiences with a personal touch. Full-service accommodations, housekeeping cabins, and tent camp available. Besides fishing, guests can enjoy watching and photographing brown bear, puffins, and eagles as well as partake in sea kayaking, fossil exploring, and clam digging. 7, 5, and 3 day trips from Kenai/Soldotna with corporate groups welcome.

Phone: 888-872-5666
davidcoray@aol.com
www.silversalmoncreek.com

STEPHAN LAKE LODGE (H&F)
Talkeetna Mountains, Alaska
Salmon/Trout/Arctic Grayling/Kodiak Bear/Brown Bear/Grizzly/Moose/ Sheep

Experience the magic. Join us at our remote, fly-in-only lodge located in the Talkeetna Mountains, 140 miles north of Anchorage. Professionally guided spin/fly fishing, salmon (King, Coho, Sockeye), Rainbow and Lake Trout, Arctic Grayling. Professionally guided sportfishing, big game hunting, and wildlife viewing. Limited to 10 guests. 3D/3N Package: $1700 per person. 10 to 12-day Spring Hunt (Kodiak/Brown Bear): $12,500 per person. Jim Bailey, Master Guide.

Phone: 907-696-2163
Fax: 907-696-2167
bbailey@ak.net

STONEY RIVER LODGE (F)
Stoney River, Alaska
King/Silver/Chum/Sockeye/Pink/Char/
Grayling/Northern Pike/Sheefish/
Lake Trout/Halibut

Private, remote, fly-in-only lodge. Specializing in daily fly-out fishing for a large variety of fish, usually fishing different locations daily. First-class accommodations, equipment and personnel. We encourage your contacting our prior clients. Free video on request. Five days fishing: $3500.

Phone: 907-696-2187
www.stoneyriverlodge.com

SUMDUM LUXURY YACHT (F)
Ketchikan to Juneau, Alaska
Salmon/Halibut

A top-of-the-line luxury yacht, the Sumdum allows you to experience the best of what Alaska offers. Guests plan their own itineraries and choose from a myriad of activities, including exploration of fjords or rivers in jet boats, water skiing, fishing for salmon or halibut, crabbing, wildlife viewing, relaxing in the hot tub, or exploring old native villages. Accommodations for eight guests with four staterooms and two full guest baths.

Phone: 800-939-2477
info@aipr.com
www.aipr.com

TALISMAN HUNTING— ALASKA (H)
Fairbanks, Alaska
Moose/Caribou/Black Bear/Brown
Bear/Mountain Goat/Dall Sheep

Some of the best quality hunting in Alaska. Moose, caribou, black bear, brown bear, mountain goat and Dall sheep. For more information, call Chuck Berg at 800-753-1139.

TIM'S TROPHY LODGE (F)
Soldotna, Alaska
Halibut/King Salmon/Coho/Sockeye/
Ling Cod/Yellow-Eye/Rainbow Trout/
Char/Pike

Selected as Alaska's #1 Fishing Destination by Times Mirror Magazines, featuring spectacular fishing, superb accommodations, culinary excellence and uncompromising customer service. Your host, Tim Berg, has pioneered local fishing techniques and has been guiding local waters for over 25 years. Nestled on the legendary Kenai River, this all-inclusive award-winning lodge is the perfect location for corporate get-togethers, couples or small groups of discriminating travelers who are looking for adventure by day and pampered comfort and luxury at night. Offering daily guided charters of both saltwater and freshwater fishing for King salmon, halibut, coho salmon, sockeye salmon, rainbow trout and ling cod, plus fly-fishing, fly-in trips, bear viewing, whale watching and wildlife tours. Featured on ESPN, ESPN2, Fox Network and TNN—your assurance of a quality vacation experience. May–Sept: 5 days/6 nights $2995.

For more information and a video, contact us:

Phone: 800-548-3474.
Fax: 707-251-9687
timmyberg@yahoo.com
www.alaskanfishing.com

WATERFALL RESORT (F)
Southeast Alaska, near Ketchikan
Legendary Sportfishing, Leading Edge Adventure

Visit a historic salmon cannery turned world-class saltwater sportfishing resort. Fish for 5 species of salmon, halibut, red snapper, and ling cod from 25-foot custom-built cabin cruisers equipped with the latest in marine electronics. While back at the resort, relax in your private lodge, cabin or townhouse, or visit the Lagoon Lounge or the restaurant to unwind. Packages include round-trip floatplane to the resort, guided fishing, meals, accommodations, and preparing fish for the trip home. Open from May–Sept. 3N/4D Packages start at $3120 per person, double occupancy. For reservations call Mike Dooley at 800-939-2477.

wfmike@ptialaska.net
www.waterfallresort.com

WEEPING TROUT SPORTS RESORT (F)
Chilkat Lake, Alaska
Cutthroat Trout/Sockeye & Coho Salmon/Dolly Varden

Getting here is pure adventure—being here is paradise. Comfortable facilities in an extraordinary setting. This 2400-acre alpine lake is accessible only by plane or jetboat through the Chilkat Bald Eagle Preserve. Trophy cutthroat trout and salmon, 8-acre golf course, brown bear and wildlife viewing. 4D/3N Packages available. Pick-up Tsirku River, air or boat landing. Debra Schnabel.

Phone: 877-94TROUT

trout@weepingtrout.com
www.weepingtrout.com

WESTWIND GUIDE SERVICE (H&F)
Eagle River, Alaska
Salmon/Trout/Northern Pike/Arctic Grayling/Brown Bear/Black Bear/ Grizzly Bear/Moose/Caribou/Wolf/ Wolverine

Hunting Southwest Alaska, Spring grizzly/brown bear hunts. Last 3 years: 20 hunters, 19 bears, many in the SCI record book. New pending # 5 & 6 SCI Grizzly Spring 2000, # 8, 9 & 14–1999. Fall guided hunts singly or in combination. Mulchatna caribou 100%, moose 80%. Guided hunts start at $2900. Unguided outfitted drop camps for moose, caribou, black bear (Caribou 98%, Moose 50%) starting at $1,500.

Phone/Fax: 907-373-2047
westwind/nayco@bigfoot.com
www.westwindguideservice.com
www.alaskaoutfittedcamps.com

WHALES RESORT (F)
Ketchikan, Alaska
Silver & Sockeye Salmon/Pike/ Rainbow Trout/Dolly Varden Trout/ Cutthroat

Battle silvers, sockeyes, and pink salmon on our deluxe 25-foot Bayliners, while Dolly Varden, rainbow, and cutthroat trout are all just a cast away through our fly-out programs. Whales Resort offers an intimate, very exclusive experience featuring upscale four-star amenities in a spectacular wilderness setting. 3N/3D packages starting at $2400. Shawn Ahnee, Resv. Mgr.

Phone: 800-531-9643.
wresort@aol.com
www.whalesresort.com

WHITE WATER OUTFITTERS (F)

Bethel, Alaska

*King/Silver/Chum/Sockeye/Pink/Char/
Grayling/Rainbow*

Truly one of the last great fishing adventures: Float fishing on the Kisaralik River. This magnificent river has water up to class III and provides both fly and spincast fishermen with some of the finest fishing to be found anywhere in the world for grayling, arctic char, rainbow, and all 5 species of salmon. Our season is from the last week of July through the second week of September. This 120-mile river float for the true outdoorsman is the adventure of a lifetime. Your tent camp trip will feature the finest most durable equipment money can buy. Our gourmet camp kitchen will produce meals with fresh seafood, steaks, chops and poultry. Two to 6 persons per float. Join Federally licensed Orvis Pro-Guide Bill Babler for this trip. Prices range to group size. All trips start from Bethel. $3550 per person and up, for this 7-day adventure. Call for info packet and video:

Phone: 800-544-0257

WILDERNESS PLACE LODGE (F)

Alaska

Fly-in Sport Fishing Lodge

Located 70 miles northwest of Anchorage on Lake Creek, Wilderness Place Lodge offers world-class angling for all 5 species of Pacific salmon, with kings over 40 lbs. commonly taken and larger fish between 50 and 60 lbs. taken each season. The 60-mile long, clear, wadeable river also has excellent fishing for native rainbow trout as well as arctic grayling. Customized raft trips of 4-7 days can also be arranged to accommodate guests desiring more remote fishing, and nearby lakes have northern pike to 15 lbs. The lodge has a capacity of 15 anglers with 3- to 7-night packages.

Phone: 907-248-4337
Fax: 907-248-1525
www.wildernessplacelodge.com

WIND RIVER CAMPS (F)

Alaska

Remote Silver Salmon Camp

The Wind River silver salmon camp is located 170 miles southwest of king salmon on a small, sand bottomed stream just a few hundred yards from tidewater. Chrome-bright silvers, fresh from the Bering Sea, arrive daily at the camp, ready for battle. These fish average over 12 lbs. with larger fish to nearly 20 lbs.! Guests can enjoy a very remote fishing experience on the rugged Alaska Peninsula while always being within 5 minutes of our first-class weatherport camp and deluxe heated cabins. Seven-day package trips from Port Heiden.

Phone: 907-245-2426
Fax: 907-248-1525
www.windriveralaska.com

YES BAY LODGE (F)

Ketchikan, Alaska

Chum/Coho/Pink/King/Sockeye Salmon

Fresh and saltwater fishing and guided tours. Yes Bay offers a variety of Alaskan experiences with an emphasis on saltwater fishing. Enjoy spin casting and fly fishing, troll for 5 species of salmon. Fish major spawning streams and hike along breathtaking views of waterfalls and hot springs. Packages include round-trip scenic floatplane between Ketchikan and the lodge, accommodations, daily maid service, meals, guided fishing, fishing tackle, bait and equipment. Package: 4N/3D $2620 per person, double occupancy.

Phone: 800-939-2477
wfmike@ptialaska.net
www.waterfallresort.com

ZACHAR BAY LODGE (F)
Kodiak Island, Alaska
Salmon/Halibut/Dolly Varden/
Rainbow Trout

Visit Zachar Bay Lodge for your Alaskan fishing or wildlife adventure. A family-run operation, Zachar Bay Lodge provides opportunities to fish for king, red and silver salmon, both in the ocean and on various rivers, as well as halibut fishing from the boats. Tour the bays and river to catch a glimpse of Alaskan wildlife: eagles, bears, seals, otter and sea birds. Don't forget to drink in the beauty of the surrounding land. Relax in the evening in modern accommodations, get your fill of a hearty meal at the dining hall, and enjoy friendly conversation with the staff. 4D/4N Package: $1900 per person. Includes round-trip airfare from Kodiak.

Phone: 800-693-2333, 907-486-4120
Fax: 907-486-4690
Zbay@ptialaska.net
www.zacharbay.com

ARIZONA
BLUE RIVER GUIDE SERVICE (H)
Safford, Arizona
Trophy Elk/Mule Deer/Coues/
Whitetail

Mid-December thru January hunting. Our hunt area is located in the White Mountains of northern Arizona and in old Mexico. All hunts are 1 on 1 and conducted during the rut for 5 days. Tags are available over the counter in Arizona or through the rancher in Mexico. For more information, contact John Bierhaus at:

Phone: 520-348-4678 or write to PO Box 703, Safford, AZ 85548.

JOHN McCLENDON & SONS GUIDE SERVICE (H)
Cottonwood, Arizona
Elk/Mule Deer/Coues Deer/
Mountain Lion

Our guide service specializes in individual trophy hunts. We offer the serious trophy hunter a chance to hunt trophy animals in the great Southwest. We gear our preseason scouting, area selection and hunt locations towards trophy selection. Our hunts are conducted from tent camps, accessible by four-wheel-drive vehicles. Hunting is done on foot or horseback.

Phone: 520-634-7957
johnmac@sedona.net

JOSH FLOWERS ARIZONA OUTFITTER/GUIDE (H)
Phoenix, Arizona
Elk/Antelope/Mule Deer/Coues/
Bighorn Sheep/Javelina/Quail

Offering fully outfitted quality hunts at very competitive prices. Early rifle bull elk $1500. Archery elk $1800. Trophy antelope $1500. Kaibab mule deer $2200. Quail hunts $250-$300 per day. Coues deer $1800. Drawing application deadline early June. Fifty percent due at time of booking. Balance to be paid on arrival. Bighorn sheep $3500. Father/Son Mule Deer Junior Hunt $1800. Javelina $800–$1000 4-day hunt. Archery, muzzleloader, rifle. Archery Desert Mule Deer $2000. 923 East Kristal Way, Phoenix, AZ 85024.

Phone: 623-587-9669

LEES FERRY ANGLERS, GUIDES & FLY SHOP (F)
Marble Canyon, Arizona
Rainbow Trout

Fish the crystal clear tail-waters of the mighty Colorado River at Lees Ferry. Established in 1989 by fly-fishing guides and IGFA World Record holders Terry Gunn, Wendy Gunn, and Russell Sullivan, Lees Ferry Anglers pride themselves on their angling expertise. Lees Ferry is a managed trout fishery, yielding 50,000 feisty Rainbow trout per mile of river. Whether you are a novice or a seasoned angler, our professional guiding staff can accommodate anyone with a keen interest in the sport. Absorb their expertise and gather an understanding of the unique methods on how to fish Lees Ferry. Guided trips include guide service, boat, and lunches. For sincere advice, availability and rates & reservations, please contact us.

Phone: 800-962-9755, 520-355-2261
Fax: 520-355-2271

anglers@leesferry.com
www.leesferry.com

UNITED STATES OUTFITTERS, ARIZONA (H)
Arizona
Elk/Mule Deer/Antelope/Coues Deer/ Sheep/Mountain Lion/Black Bear

USO has built a tremendous reputation in the hunting industry by hunting the best areas of the Rockies. By guaranteed private land tags as well as draw tags, USO's clients harvest more trophy-class animals than any other outfitter in the nation each year. Archery, muzzleloader, and rifle hunts available. USO handles all the applications through their "professional licensing service" and fronts much of the license cost to their hunters in order to apply to multiple quality areas to have the best chance of obtaining a real trophy hunt. Very comfortable accommodations, great food. Normally no horseback required. Hunt costs are $3450.

Phone: 800-845-9929
www.huntuso.com

ARKANSAS

ADAM'S STRIPER GUIDE SERVICE (F)
Beaver Lake, Arkansas
Stripers

Guided fishing tour with Guide Junior Adams. Thirty years experience and the latest fishing equipment ensures you will have the best shot at catching that big one. All bait and tackle furnished. Located just 90 minutes from Branson, Missouri, and Bass Pro Shop. Full-day trip

(8 hrs): $325. Half-day trip (5 hrs.): $225.

Phone: 501-359-3733

BEAVER GUIDE SERVICE & LODGING (F)
Eureka Springs, Arkansas
Trophy Stripers/Rainbow Trout/ Walleye

Year-round trophy striper fishing at its best! In the past 10 years, we have caught over 75,000 pounds of stripers,—1,835 over 20 pounds and 277 over 30 pounds. Our lodge is located close to White River and Beaver Lake. Come and stay with us to see the beauty of the Ozarks. While you are here plan to stay an extra day or two to float the river and trout fish. We have trout, walleye and striper guides available year round. Daily rates: 4 hrs., $225; 6 hrs., $275; 8 hrs., $325. Rooms for $60 for two.

Phone: 501-253-5048 (Gene Chapman)
beaverguidelodge@arkansas.net
www.beaverguideservice.com

BUFFALO RIVER OUTFITTERS (H&F)
St. Joe, Arkansas
Turkey/Deer/Elk/Black Bear/ Smallmouth Bass/Brownies/ Rainbow Trout

Spring and fall hunting. Over 2000 acres of lush hunting in the Arkansas Ozark Mountain region full of wild turkey and deer. Elk hunts on the Buffalo River National Park (permit required). Day packages starting at $225 per person. Fully furnished rustic log cabins available for overnight stays starting at $90 per night. Fishing dur-

ing the Spring and Summer on the Buffalo National River and the White River. Day trips starting at $90 per person.

Phone: 800-582-2244
bro1@alltel.net
www.buffaloriveroutfitters.com

JUST FISHIN' GUIDES (F)
Northwest Arkansas
Trout/Bass

Based out of northwest Arkansas with year-round fishing, we fish for everything from smallmouth and largemouth bass to the White, Norfork, and Little Red Rivers' trophy rainbow, brook, brown and cutthroat trout. Whether it is fly fishing for a trophy trout from our driftboat or stalking a wary stream smallmouth, our guide service will do our best to put you on that special fish. Guide service $250 per day for 1-2 persons, equipment and lunch included. Accommodations can be set up for any budget.

Phone: 501-273-0276
kenrice@tcac.net
www.justfishinguides.com

CALIFORNIA

DELTA HOUSEBOAT RENTALS (F)
Stockton, California
Black Bass/Catfish/Stripers/Crappie/ Sturgeon/Crawdads

Enjoy the ultimate floating fish camp . . . a luxury houseboat rental from Forever Resorts' Delta Houseboat Rentals! Fish from sunup to sundown without the hassle of a crowded boat ramp—just step off the back deck and into your fishing boat! Each houseboat sleeps 10 in five queen beds and is equipped with all the amenities of home, including gas grill, coffee maker, full-size range, microwave, TV, VCR, central A/C and 2 refrigerators. We even provide linens and pots and pans! It's the perfect floating fish camp! Rates start at $995 for 4 days/3 nights midweek . . . that's $95 per person for 4 days! 11580 West 8 Mile Road, Stockton, CA 95219.

Phone: 800-255-5561 or visit www.foreverresorts.com/HFD

MOCCASIN POINT MARINA (F)
Lake Don Pedro, California
Largemouth Bass/Smallmouth Bass/ Stripers/Crappie/Rainbow Trout/ Kokanee Salmon/Bluegill

Enjoy the ultimate floating fish camp . . . a luxury houseboat rental on Lake Don Pedro from Forever Resorts' Moccasin Point Marina! Fish from sunup to sundown without the hassle of a crowded boat ramp—just step off the back deck and into your fishing boat! Each houseboat sleeps 10 in five queen beds and is equipped with all the amenities of home, including gas grill, coffee maker, full-size range, microwave, TV, VCR, central A/C and 2 refrigerators. We even provide linens and pots and pans! It's the perfect floating fish camp! Rates start at $995 for 4 days/3 nights midweek . . . that's $95 per person for 4 days! 11405 Jacksonville Road, Jamestown, CA 95327.

Phone: 800-255-5561 or visit www.foreverresorts.com/HFD

TRINITY LAKE RESORTS (F)
Trinity Center, California
Largemouth Bass/Smallmouth Bass/ Stripers/Crappie/Rainbow Trout/ Kokanee Salmon

Enjoy the ultimate floating fish camp . . . a luxury houseboat rental from Forever Resorts' Trinity Lake Resorts! Fish from sunup to sundown without the hassle of a crowded boat ramp—just step off the back deck and into your fishing boat! Each houseboat sleeps 10 in five queen beds and is equipped with all the amenities of home, including gas grill, coffee maker, full-size range, microwave, TV, VCR, central A/C and 2 refrigerators. We even provide linens and pots and pans! It's the perfect floating fish camp! Rates start at $995 for 4 days/3 nights midweek . . . that's $95 per person for 4 days! 45810 State Highway 3, Trinity Center, CA 96091.

Phone: 800-255-5561 or visit www.foreverresorts.com/HFD

COLORADO

ARCHERY UNLIMITED OUTFITTERS (H)
Southwestern Colorado
Elk/Mule Deer

Horse pack trips into the scenic San Juan Mountains. Offering deluxe fully guided and drop camps for archery, muzzleloading and rifle seasons. Licensed, bonded and fully insured, #1148. Marshall Ledford, 878 Quarter Horse Rd., Durango, CO 81301.

Phone: 970-259-3813 www.archeryunlimited.com

BAR H OUTFITTERS (H&F)
Northwest Colorado
Elk/Mule Deer/Trout

First-class, full-time professional outfitter offering pack-in tent camp hunts or cabins in GMU 12 & 24, home to one of Colorado's largest elk herds. Excellent staff of guides, cooks and wranglers work hard to meet the needs of our guests. Summer and Fall fishing trips are also available on the White River and in the Flattops Wilderness Area. Permittee in White River and Routt National Forests. Fully licensed, insured and bonded, #1913. Seven-day trips: Fully Guided $3000, Cabin Hunts $2000, Drop Camps $1200. Fishing trips, $200 per day. Randy & Jeanne Horne.

Phone: 800-230-HUNT
jhorne@flattops.net
www.barhoutfitters.com

BILL DVORAK FISHING & RAFTING EXPEDITIONS (F)
Colorado and Wyoming
Trophy Rainbows/ Browns/Cutthroats

Outfitting since 1969. Cast yourself in a different direction on a customized float fishing trip with Dvorak's. We offer trips on some of the wildest and most productive trout waters in the West. Whichever river you choose, let the professional fishing guides take you there. Excellent "Gold Medal," "Blue Ribbon" and world-class rivers like the Gunnison, North Platte, Arkansas, Dolores, and Middle Fork of the Salmon rivers to choose from. Trip lengths from half-day to 4 days of hot fishing action. Rafts will carry maximum two anglers at a cost from $105 to $300 per day per angler. Multiday trips will provide all meals, boating equipment and one guide per raft. Transportation air/land and tips not included.

Phone: 800-824-3795
www.dvorakexpeditions.com

BLACK MOUNTAIN RANCH (H)
McCoy, Colorado
Elk/Mule Deer

Quality ranch hunts at Black Mountain Ranch in McCoy, Colorado. Over 1000 private acres surrounded by BLM and National Forest land in the heart of some of the best Mule Deer and Elk terrain in the state. Comfortable accommodations, great food, experienced guides, gentle horses. We offer 5 days guided combination hunts. Bonded and insured, #1343.

Phone: 800-283-8984

BLUE CREEK OUTFITTERS (H)
Colorado Trophy Unit 61
Elk/Mule Deer/Bear/ Mountain Lion/Turkey

Quality hunts in Colorado's Trophy Unit 61, one of Colorado's premiere hunting areas. Our camps offer trophy hunting, limited hunters, home-cooked meals, comfortable camping facilities, qualified guides, and unsurpassed scenery. Rifle, archery, and muzzleloading hunts. Bonded and insured, #314. Scott and Debbie Dillon.

Phone: 970-864-2250
www.unit61.com

BUFFALO HORN RANCH (H&F)
Northwest Colorado
Pheasant/Huns/Chukar/Trout

First-class guest ranch, encompassing over 20,000 acres in cowboy country! In summer, enjoy our six-day vacation packages. Delight in horseback adventures, cattle drives, clay shooting, hiking, swimming, fishing and BBQs. Our chefs prepare fabulous food and you are sure to enjoy our cozy log lodge and beautiful new duplex cabins. In fall, come for Orvis-endorsed upland bird hunting with our experienced guides and eager hunting dogs. Three-day packages available. Lic. # 1616.

Phone: 877-878-5450 (toll free)
Fax: 970-878-4088
www.buffalohorn.com

BUGLE MOUNTAIN OUTFITTERS (H&F)
Southwest Colorado
Trout/Elk/Deer/Black Bear/Mountain Lion/Merriam Turkey/Grouse

We get started in the spring, hunting Merriam Turkey. After summer rolls around, we start our Summer Pack trips into the San Juan Mountains trying to catch the ever-elusive brook trout, which we cook out over the fire for dinner. After summer, we start our high country and private property hunts for Elk, Mule Deer, and Black Bear. We also offer Mountain Lion hunts in the late fall and early spring. We practice quality, not quantity, only hunting four people per camp. We can customize the trip to meet your needs. We offer deluxe guided camps, deluxe drop, and drop camps. We are licensed, bonded and insured. We hunt in game management units 74, 75, 77, 751 and 771.

Phone: 970-884-2730
elk@buglemtnoutfitters.com
www.buglemtnoutfitters.com

CAPITOL PEAK OUTFITTERS (H&F)
Carbondale, Colorado
Trout/Bear/Mule Deer/Elk

Capitol Peak Outfitters and Aspen Wilderness Outfitters offer a wide range of summer horseback adventures near Aspen, Colorado. Short-duration, day and overnight wilderness trips for fishing and tremendous back country scenery are available. Fall brings great color rides or guided drop camp archery and black powder hunts for elk and deer. Rifle guided and drop camp hunts run from mid-October to mid-November. Trophy-class mule deer are available. Guided archery and black powder hunts pack into a remote camp deep inside the Hunter-Frying Pan Wilderness with experienced bugle guides capable of coaxing big bulls into short range.

Phone: 970-963-0211
capitolpk@aol.com
www.capitolpeak.com

CIRCLE K RANCH (H)
Southwest Colorado Rockies
Elk/Mule Deer/Black Bear

Affordable quality hunts since 1961 in the spectacular San Juan National Forest. Stay in our historic lodge or modern cabins, or book a drop camp pack-in hunt. Guided, unguided, archery, muzzleloader, or rifle hunts. Summer months: cabin rentals, trail rides, overnight pack trips, horseback, native trout adventures, great home cooking and more. Family owned/operated. 27758 Hwy 145, Dolores, CO 81323.

Phone: 970-562-3808 (hunts)
Summer 970-562-3826,
    800-477-6381
ckranch2@fone.net
www.sportsmansdream.com

COLORADO TROPHIES (H)
Colorado Rockies
Elk/Mule Deer/Black Bear/Mountain Lion

Quality hunting experience on 30,000 acres of private ranch land with spectacular views, home to abundant herds of elk and mule deer. We hunt archery (50% success), muzzleloader (75% success), and rifle (70% success). Includes: Fully guided 2 on 1 hunts, field care of meat and trophy, first-class lodge accommodations with all meals, transportation to and from airport and in the field with 4x4s & ATVs, trout fishing on our private lake. Rates: Archery hunts $2450–$4450. Rifle hunts $3450–$5950. Lic. #1782.

Phone: 970-327-4678 (Tom Colander)
www.coloradotrophies.com

COULTER LAKE GUEST RANCH AND OUTFITTERS (H&F)
White River National Forest, Colorado Rockies
Elk/Mule Deer/Turkey/Fly Fishing

Hunt out the front door of your cabin, or on ATV or horseback. Ranch is at 8100 ft. elevation. We supply your cabin with three full meals per day. Will pack out game at extra charge. Sample hunting package: 5 days minimum, cabins and meals, $1100 per person; with a horse and wrangler, $1600 per person. Trout fishing in front of cabin year-round. Lic. 73. in Unit 33.

Phone: 800-858-3046
coulter@sopris.net

D BAR G OUTFITTERS (H)
Durango, Colorado
Elk/Deer/Bear

Class A ranch hunt in Durango, Colorado. 2500 acres of private land bordered by a wildlife refuge. This ranch holds several resident elk herds as well as migrating elk. High success on elk, bear and deer. 5-day hunt, heated cabins, horses, professional guides. All meals and packing of all game are included in the price of $2,500 rifle and $1,800 muzzleloader and bow. Summer cabins and horseback riding. Bonded and insured, #1704. Dayson Goetz.

Phone: 970-385-6888
www.sportsmansdream.com/dbarg/

DRAGONFLY ANGLERS (H&F)
Gunnison, Colorado
Elk/Mule Deer/Black Bear/Rainbow/Brook/Brown/Cutthroat

Big game hunting Colorado game management unit 521, private land and Gunnison National Forest. Hunt for Elk, Mule Deer and Black Bear. Quality Ranch hunt packages start at $2500 for 5-day rifle hunt and $2250 for 6-day archery hunts. Fly fishing the Gunnison River Basin, experienced guides for the novice to expert angler. Fish for Rainbow, Brown, Cut-throat, and Brook Trout. World-fa-mous tail-waters such as the Taylor River for the possibility of a 20-lb. Rainbow or the Black Canyon of the Gunnison for trophy Rainbow, and Brown Trout. Bonded and insured with special use permits from USDA-Forest Service, USDI-BLM and NPS. Contact us.

For hunting: 970-349-9836
For fishing: 970-349-1228
barkranch@freeze.com
www.dragonflyanglers.com

FERRO'S BLUE MESA OUTFITTERS (H&F)
Gunnison, Colorado
Elk/Mule Deer/Fishing Trips

Fishing and hunting paradise in Gunnison, Colorado area. Blue Mesa Lake pontoon trips for spring trophy Macinaw in spring, and salmon and trout in summer. Stream fish in remote areas for that bonus trout. Special guided elk and mule deer hunts in the remote luxury 3-story cabin (on 160 acres/private property) surrounded by National Forest in Unit 66. Also great for corporate outings, weddings or family gatherings. Call about GMU 54 Fall hunts. Summer horseback rides, cabins, boating groups and indi-viduals at Blue Mesa. Lic. #996.

Phone: 970-641-4671
ferrobluemesa@dmea.net
www.coloradoadventures.net

IRON MOUNTAIN LODGE & RESORT (H&F)
Northern Colorado Rockies
Elk/Mule Deer/Fly & Lake Fishing

Snowmobiles, fourwheeling, hiking and more. Hunt some of the best wildlife terrain the Rockies have to of-fer. Secluded stream and lake fishing. Guided and unguided hunts and fish-ing trips. Enjoy an experience you will never forget! Bring your camera! Get 3 home-cooked meals per day, a spacious log cabin, and friendly hosts. Come and visit us soon, where your outdoor dreams come true!

Phone: 970-290-4148, 308-874-4589

KING MOUNTAIN RANCH (F)
Granby, Colorado
Trout

High in the Rocky Mountains, the King Ranch is completely surrounded by the Arapaho National Forest. Our private lake has some of the largest brook trout you'll ever reel in, up to 22 inches. And only a short distance from the ranch you can test some of Colorado's finest Gold Medal stream fishing. Guided fly fishing trips also available. We're the ideal family vaca-tion. Conference facilities. 6-night stay during summer months: $1795 per person, double occupancy; chil-dren (3–12) $1350 per person, double occupancy. John Fisher, General Man-ager.

Phone: 800-476-5464
Fax: 970-887-9511
www.kingmtnranch.com

MOTHERWELL LODGE (H&F)
Steamboat Springs, Colorado
Elk/Mule Deer/Rainbow/Brown/ Brook/Cutthroat Trout

The Motherwell Lodge is located near Steamboat Springs, Colorado.

Luxurious lodging, sumptuous cuisine and top-drawer service. World-class angling. All private waters. Featured in the *Flyfisherman Magazine* July 2000 article, "Catch Monster Trout in Hog Pens." Trophy elk and deer hunting.

Toll free: 877-HUNTFISH

(Rob Raley)

www.westernstatesoutdoors.com

PIKES PEAK OUTFITTERS (H)
Woodland Park, Colorado
Elk/Mule Deer/Whitetail Deer/
Antelope/Turkey

Quality ranch hunts along with wilderness tent camps in Colorado, Kansas, Nebraska and Texas. Our professional guides will take you into territory that is game rich and scenery that is unsurpassed by none. With private ranches and thousands of BLM and National Forest acres, the guides will take you on a 2 on 1 hunt you will never forget. Comfortable accommodations, great home-cooked meals, and a friendly staff will make your stay more pleasurable. Our 7-day hunt packages range from $2500–$6500. Combination hunts are also available. Members of the Rocky Mountain Elk Foundation, North American Hunting Club, and also recognized by the top magazine publications in the country.

Phone: 800-748-2885

pikespeak@pikespeakhunt.com

www.pikespeakhunt.com

ROCK CREEK OUTFITTERS (H)
Rand, Colorado
Elk/Deer/Antelope/Moose

A 2257-acre cattle ranch high in the Colorado Rockies, bordered by the Routt National Forest, that offers quality hunts for elk, deer, antelope and moose. Elk and deer hunts are primarily from stands or blinds, catering to the mature or less physically fit hunter. Lodging is in the large ranch house converted to a hunting lodge with private bedrooms. Nonhunters and spouses are welcome. Small hunting groups of four or six hunters per season help make this a pleasant, higher-kill-percentage value for your dollar hunt. Hunts are as follows: 5D/6N first season elk hunt: $2250; 5D/6N 2nd, 3rd or 4th season elk hunt: $1950; 5D/6N moose hunts: $3000; 3D/4N antelope hunts: $750; 5D/6N deer hunts: $1800. All lodgings and meals are furnished and we offer one guide per two hunters.

Phone: 970-723-4211

bobethompson@yahoo.com

www.hometown.aol.com/
rockcreekhunting

ROCKY MOUNTAIN RANCHES (H)
Northwest Colorado
Elk/Deer/Antelope

Rocky Mountain Ranches is proud to offer you the opportunity to hunt some of the finest ranches in northwest Colorado. This area is famous for its extraordinary big-game hunting. All of our ranches are managed to provide and maintain superb trophy hunting. Because we allow only a limited number of hunters each year, your chance for success greatly increases. Bow, muzzleloader, and rifle hunts are available. Both individuals and groups are welcome. All hunts are on a trespass fee basis and are nonguided. Price ranges from $900–$1750 pp. Licensed, bonded, insured, #1543. Member, Rocky Mountain Elk Foundation, and Approved Outfitter, North American Hunting Club.

Phone: 303-286-8656 (Larry Bishop)

SAMUELSON OUTFITTERS (H)
Colorado Rockies
Elk/Mule Deer

Quality wilderness hunts in a roadless, nonmotorized vehicle area southwest of Rocky Mountain National Park. Over 80,000 square acres of pristine National Forest land in the heart of some of the best elk and mule deer hunting in Colorado. Comfortable camps with great food, experienced guides, gentle horses. In the business for over 30 years. 5-day/2 on 1 combination hunts $3200. Drop camp $1600. Bonded, insured, #729. Richard and Cathy Samuelson.

Phone: 888-346-7978
samuelsonoutfitters@coweblink.net
www.samuelsonoutfitters.com

SANTA FE OUTFITTERS (H&F)
Headwaters of the Navajo River, Southern Colorado
Elk

Exclusive private acreage of world-class elk hunting territory in the headwaters of the Navajo River in south central Colorado. Ringed by spectacular 13,000-foot peaks, this private ranch has rarely been hunted in the past 36 years and has at least 2000 elk residing on its 20,000 acres, with many Boone and Crockett bulls. Each hunt includes world-class fly fishing

on the Navajo River and alpine lakes for German brown and cutthroat trout. During your hunt you will receive first-class accommodations, gourmet food and expert guiding. Owners: Bob King and Clay Allison.

Phone: 505-474-9393

UNITED STATES OUTFITTERS, COLORADO (H)
Colorado
Sheep/Moose/Mountain Goat

USO has built a tremendous reputation in the hunting industry by hunting the best areas of the Rockies. By guaranteed private land tags as well as draw tags, USO's clients harvest more trophy-class animals than any other outfitter in the nation each year. Archery, muzzleloader, and rifle hunts available. USO handles all the applications through their "professional licensing service" and fronts much of the license cost to their hunters in order to apply to multiple quality areas to have the best chance of obtaining a real trophy hunt. Very comfortable accommodations, great food.

Phone: 800-845-9929
www.huntuso.com

WING SHADOW RANCH (F)
Colorado Rockies
Rainbow/Cutthroat Trout

Colorado's premiere fly fishing school and trips. "School" has never been more fun! You'll have a blast learning to improve your fly-fishing skills with an experienced and charismatic Master Guide in a small group setting. Your "classroom" waters will include lake, stream and river in the Rocky Mountains, as you practice your new skills fishing for trout. Individualized instruction based on your skill level; learning about casting, entomology, equipment, reading waters, increasing productivity of your fly selection, trout behavior, wading safety and much more! Enjoy spectacular views from our first-class lodge accommodations with all meals. Transportation to and from airport. Fishing equipment rental available. Rates: $595 per person.

Phone: 970-327-4050 (Tom Colander)
www.wingshadowranch.com

CONNECTICUT

WESTPORT OUTFITTERS (F)
Westport, Connecticut
Saltwater Flyfishing & Light Tackle Spinfishing

Come fish the legendary Norwalk Islands with Orvis endorsed Master Guide, Capt. Jeff Northrop and his fleet of flats guides. Experience true Northeast flats fishing for striped bass, bluefish, bonito, and false albacore from the decks of our Hewes and Maverick skiffs. Our pro shop and docks are located on the Saugatuck River, only 10 minutes from the prime, protected fishing grounds of Connecticut's Long Island Sound. Conveniently located 45 minutes north of Manhattan and one hour south of Hartford. For pricing and info please contact us.

Phone: 203-226-1915
godzilla41@aol.com
www.saltwater-flyfishing.com

FLORIDA

CAPTAIN DAN MALZONE (F)
Tampa, Florida
Redfish/Tarpon/Trout/Snook

Fabulous year-round fly and light-tackle fishing on the west coast of Florida flats for redfish, trout, snook and giant tarpon. Three world-record tarpon on fly.

Phone: 813-831-4052
capt.dan.malzone@worldnet.att.net
www.home.att.net/~capt.dan.alzone

CAPTAIN TED WILSON (F)
Islamorada, Florida Keys
Bonefish/Permit/Tarpon/Redfish/Snook

Islamorada . . . where it all began. This magical island and the people who fish it have been pioneering what the rest of the world now refers to as "flats fishing" for fifty years. Undeniably the largest year-round bonefish on Earth. Huge permit. The world's most famous clear-water sight fishing tarpon fishery, March through July. Everglades National Park is just minutes away, if redfish, sea trout or snook are your favorite. Quality light spinning rods or fly fishing gear are the choice and provided. Full day trip $395. Half day $295. Rates are all-inclusive for up to 2 anglers, $100 for third angler. Come see what everybody's been talking about for all these years.

Phone: 305-664-9463
capt_ted_wilson@hotmail.com

C.B.'s SALTWATER OUTFITTERS (F)
Siesta Key, Sarasota, Florida
Tarpon/Redfish/Spotted Sea Trout/
Snook/Pompano/Cobia/Jack Crevalle

Located on beautiful, laid-back Siesta Key, we offer excellent fly and light-tackle angling for tarpon from May to July in the clear, inshore Gulf of Mexico, and off nearby Boca Grande country of Sarasota Bay and the estuary of Charlotte Harbor for redfish, spotted sea trout and snook. Pompano, cobia, tarpon (in season). Excellent sightfishing for snook at night. The fall, September and October, can be excellent months to fish. And in the winter months, large schools of jack crevalle exceeding 15 lbs. will surely test your limits on light tackle in out back bays and on the flats. Complete Orvis shop, fly-casting clinics and fishing seminars offered. Ask for Aledia, Chris or Doug. 1249 Stickney Point Road, Siesta Key, Sarasota, FL 34242.

Phone: 941-349-4400
info@cbsoutfitters.com
www.cbsoutfitters.com

CHARTER BOAT KALEX (F)
Islamorada, Florida Keys
Sailfish/Marlin/Tuna/Dolphin/Tarpon

30 years fishing experience in Islamorada and worldwide. Many world-record accomplishments. Enjoy billfishing, reef fishing, kite fishing and wreck fishing. All day: $850 per day, up to 6 passengers. Everything included except food and drink.

Nov–May: sailfish, reef, wreck and kite fishing; May–Oct: reef, wreck and dolphin fishing. May–July: tarpon fishing. Contact Captain Alex Adler and experience the joy of the world-famous Kalex Charter Boat. 48-ft. custom, twin diesel powered. Fly fishing also available.

Phone: 305-852-5084

CHEECA LODGE (F)
Islamorada, Florida Keys
Tarpon/Bonefish/Permit/Sailfish/
Grouper/Wahoo/Snapper/Marlin/Tuna

Cheeca Lodge is the "Sport Fishing Capital of the World." This 27-acre, luxury oceanfront resort offers world-class fishing for trophy gamefish: tarpon, bonefish and permit in the quiet waters of the Everglades and Florida Bay, or the fast-paced action of offshore fishing for magnificent sailfish, marlin, tuna, wahoo and more. Cheeca Lodge is home of the George Bush/Cheeca Lodge Bonefish Tournament held each fall, and the Presidential Sailfish Tournament held each January. This full-service, destination resort has something for every member of the family, including the brand new Avanyu Spa & Fitness Center, water sports, diving, tennis, golf, and an award-winning children's program. Ask about our Grand Slam Fishing Package, which does not include fishing charter fees. However, the lodge's concierge can make those arrangements for you.

Phone: 800-327-2888

EVERGLADES ANGLER (F)
Naples, Florida

Snook/Tarpon/Redfish/Speckled Sea Trout/Pompano/Snapper

The Everglades Angler, located in Naples, is an Orvis full-line dealer and outfitter and is headquarters for the Everglades Angler guide service. The Everglades Angler guide team is comprised of 14 of the top guides in South Florida and will not only put you on fish but can help educate and instruct with courtesy and patience. The tidal estuaries of Southwest Florida's mangrove coast are the life-blood of the Everglades National Park and the 10,000 Islands and produce some of the finest and most unique fishing in the world. Snook, tarpon, redfish, trout, pompano and other saltwater species inhabit this unspoiled wilderness. Fishing can be good all year, although it peaks in the early summer through fall. September and October can be especially productive and can produce excellent numbers of fish. Everglades Angler's newest service "Fishing Worldwide" continues to offer destination fishing trips around the world. Fly fishing school and tying clinics also offered. 810 12th Avenue South, Naples, FL 34102.

Phone: 800-573-4749, 941-262-8228
mail@evergladesangler.com
www.evergladesangler.com

EXTREME LIGHT TACKLE SPORTFISHING (F)
Jupiter, Florida
Sailfish/Shark/King Mackerel/ Snook/Tarpon

"Sportfishing on the Edge" with Capt. George LaBonte. Southeast Florida offers unparalleled variety in bluewater sportfishing! With over 20 species of hard-charging game fish available year-round, no other destination can compete. Let popular radio talk show "Florida Sportsman Magazine Live" host Capt. George introduce you to a few of sunny Florida's bluewater residents. The *Edge* is a custom-built 25-foot open fisherman designed for "extreme hands-on fishing." Your skipper has 25 years experience guiding clients around the globe. He has been featured in every national magazine for fishing including *Florida Sportsman*, *Saltwater Sportsman*, *Marlin*, and *Sport Fishing*. He is author of *Fishing for Sailfish* and has guided clients to numerous IGFA world record catches. Cost for the boat is $425 for a full day and $300 for the half day. Call for availability.

Phone: 561-746-0032
fishingtheedge@yahoo.com

THE FLORIDIAN SPORTS CLUB (F)
Welaka, Florida
Freshwater Bass

A fisherman's paradise! Located right on the historic St. John's River. An exclusive retreat with the best bass fishing anywhere in Florida. Main lodge, guest cottages, swimming pool. Casual. Relaxed. Natural. 3D/4N Package: $1466 for two people. Includes 3 days fishing with guide, boat, motor, and meals.

Phone: 904-467-2181 (Mike Ballard)

FREE JUMPER CHARTERS (F)
Southeast Florida
Light Tackle Tarpon/Snook

Enjoy world-class tarpon and snook fishing in the Sailfish Capitol of the World, Stuart, Florida. These fisheries usually begin in the latter part of May and continue through the summer until the first cold front, usually in October. Fly fishing, spinning or conventional with live bait or artificial. It all works! Chartered by the day. Up to 3 anglers. $300 half; $400 full. Capt. David Fawcett.

Phone: 561-283-7787
dfawcett@ix.netcom.com

HAMPTON & HAMPTON GUIDE SERVICE (H&F)
Melbourne, Florida
Alligator/Hog/Turkey/Duck/Tarpon/ Largemouth Bass/Spotted Sea Trout/ Redfish

We do year-round bow and rifle hunts for alligator: an all-inclusive 2-day hunt is $1750 per person and includes meals, motel, license and guide. We also offer hog, Osceola turkey and duck hunts; fishing trips for tarpon, redfish, trout and largemouth bass; some fly fishing; and bluewater trips. We are located on the coast of east central Florida in Melbourne, one hour from Orlando, forty miles south of Kennedy Space Center, and five miles from local beaches.

Phone: 321-242-1012, 800-948-4339
www.hhgatorhunts.com

OFFSHORE FISHING WITH SATISFACTION GUARANTEED CHARTERS (F)
Naples/Marco Island, Florida
Snook/Tarpon/Redfish/Trout/Shark/ Barracuda/Snapper/Grouper/Cobia/ Drum/Permit/Pompano

Offshore fishing in the Gulf of Mexico. 3 days offshore fishing and 4 nights accommodations with three shore lunches included. Fish the Gulf of Mexico aboard a custom built 24-ft. center console that can comfortably fish up to 6 passengers. Bottom fish over wrecks for grouper, snapper, cobia, shark, and permit or troll along in search of king mackerel and barracuda. Equipped with a head and T-top for shade, this boat makes those all-day trips enjoyable for everyone. Springtime shark fishing is a thrilling experience! Each day of fishing includes a shore lunch and beverages. Alcohol may be purchased with advance notice. Hotel accommodations are conveniently located just minutes from Naples's wonderful nightlife and world-class restaurants. Offshore fishing package price April 16–Dec. 20, $2000/person, double occupancy; Dec. 21–April 15, $2200/person, double occupancy. Please call Capt. Brien Spina

Phone: 941-642-9779 for booking reservations and information
captbrien@aol.com
www.marcoislandcharters.com

PELICAN COVE RESORT (F)
Islamorada, Florida Keys
Bonefish/Tarpon/Permit/Snook/ Redfish/Sea Trout

Enjoy excellent back-country fishing with some of Florida's most experienced guides. Spectacular ocean views are the perfect backdrop for Pelican Cove's tastefully furnished rooms and suites. All rooms have a spacious private balcony overlooking the ocean, coffee makers, cable TV and refrigerators; 27 have full kitchens. Guests not only enjoy world-class fishing but also tennis, water sports, a freshwater pool, oceanfront Jacuzzi, sandy beach, floating sunbathing/diving dock, a cabana bar and café, and free continental breakfast daily. For reservations, call toll-free:

Phone: 800-445-4690
info@pcove.com
www.pcove.com

PRO FISHING GUIDE
SERVICE (F)
Bartow, Florida
Catch & Release Bass Fishing

Located in Central Florida's Polk County with its 600-plus lakes. Many bass of 15 lbs. and over have been caught and released by our clients. A variety of accommodations conveniently located near Disney World and the beaches. Only state-of-the-art bass boats and top-of-the-line equipment are used. $275 for two people per day. Live bait, licenses and gratuities not included. Dave Hoy.

Phone: 800-695-4227

ROLAND MARTIN'S MARINA
& RESORT (F)
Clewiston, Florida
Largemouth Bass/Bluegill/Crappie

Fish out of world-famous Roland Martin's Marina and Resort on legendary Lake Okeechobee—the world's best bass fishing with the world's best guides (largest freshwater guide service in the world). Lake Okeechobee is world famous for its tremendous largemouth bass, bluegill, and crappie fishing. At Roland Martin's you may choose from a variety of comfortable accommodations. The motel offers spacious rooms or deluxe efficiencies. Or you may prefer a luxurious apartment in the beautiful condominiums. Two heated swimming pools are provided for recreation and relaxation. Winter and summer rates available.

Phone: 800-473-6766
www.rolandmartinmarina.com

SATISFACTION GUARANTEED
FISHING CHARTERS (F)
10,000 Islands, Marco Island, Florida
Backwater and flats fishing

3 days backwater fishing and 4 nights accommodations with three shore lunches included. Enjoy fishing the backwaters and estuaries of the Ten Thousand Islands in search of giant snook, tarpon, redfish, trout, pompano

and snapper. You will be intrigued by the scenic landscapes that this nature preserve has to offer. Aboard your journey you will see dolphin, manatee, osprey, and many other breath-taking sights. Whether you prefer casting a hand-tied fly or pitching live bait against the mangrove shores, we can accommodate all your backwater fishing needs. Each day of fishing includes a shore lunch and beverages. Alcohol may be purchased with advance notice. Hotel accommodations are conveniently located just minutes from Naples's wonderful nightlife and world-class restaurants. Backwater fishing package price: April 16–Dec. 20, $1700/person, double occupancy; Dec. 21–April 15, $1900/person, double occupancy; Please call for reservations and information.

Phone: 941-642-9779
captbrien@aol.com
www.marcoislandcharters.com

SOUTH SEAS RESORT (F)
Captiva Island, Florida
Snook/Redfish/Grouper/Snapper/ Tarpon/Kingfish/Cobia/Shark

South Seas Resort sits on 330 acres of the most beautiful land on the tip of Captiva Island, Florida, offering offshore and inshore fishing. With 600 units ranging from hotel rooms to 4-bedroom homes, plus 18 swimming pools, 18 tennis courts, a 9-hole golf course, a driving range, 2½ miles of pristine beach, 5 restaurants, 9 retail boutiques, child and adult recreation programs, 2 marinas and water sports ranging from a fishing dock to sailing charters, South Seas Resort is the ultimate vacation destination resort.

Phone: 1-800-CAPTIVA
www.south-seas-resort.com

WHATEVER'S BITIN' SPORTFISHING CHARTERS (F)
Jupiter Inlet, Florida
Sailfish/Dolphin/Wahoo/Kingfish/ Snapper/Grouper/Snook/Tarpon

With the warm Gulf Stream waters only 3 miles away, the fishing here is always great. We have year-round fishing, with January being the top month for sailfish. Spring brings kingfish, dolphin and bottom fishing to the top of the list. Summer time then allows for the snook and tarpon run. June, July and August *are* the top months for these species. *All fish are released.* Great restaurants and lodging are all within minutes of my dock. Price: $275 half-day; $500 full day. Capt. Mike Linville.

Phone: 561-748-4873
www.whateversbitin.com

GEORGIA

LAKE LANIER HOUSEBOAT RENTALS (F)
Buford, Georgia
Largemouth Bass/Stripers/Crappie/ Catfish/Bluegill

Enjoy the ultimate floating fish camp . . . a luxury houseboat rental from Forever Resorts' Lake Lanier Houseboat Rentals! Fish from sunup to sundown without the hassle of a crowded boat ramp—just step off the back deck and into your fishing boat! Each houseboat sleeps 10 in five queen beds and is equipped with all the amenities of home, including gas grill, coffee maker, full-size range, microwave, TV, VCR, central A/C and 2 refrigerators. We even provide the linens and pots and pans! It's the perfect floating fish camp! Rates starting at $995 for 4 days/3 nights midweek . . . that's $95 per person for 4 days! 6900 Holiday Road, Buford, GA 30518.

Phone: 800-255-5561

www.foreverresorts.com/HFD

THE LODGE ON LITTLE ST. SIMONS ISLAND (F)
Little St. Simons Island, Georgia
Redfish/Sea Trout/Flounder

Little St. Simons Island offers 10,000 acres of pristine, untouched wilderness and miles of shoreline and tidal creeks along the Georgia coast. Accessible only by boat, there are never more than 30 overnight guests on the island at any time. Recipient of the "Best Small Hotel in North America" 2000 Conde Nast Award. Along with excellent fishing, there is a variety of outdoor activities and interpretive educational programs ranging from bird watching and canoeing to "Summer Fun for Families" programs. Peak fishing on the island runs from mid-August through early November. The local waters abound with redfish, sea trout and other game species. A nature lover's paradise, with a degree of solitude that is becoming increasingly hard to find, the Lodge on Little St. Simons Island offers a unique and memorable vacation experience. Information about the Private Hunt Club is available upon request.

Toll-free: 888-733-5774

www.LittleStSimonsIsland.com

HAWAII

SOUTH POINT SAFARIS (H)

Kealakekua, Hawaii
Trophy Mouflon Sheep/Wild Boar/ Vancouver Bull/Bison/Rio Grande Turkey

South Point, on the Big Island of Hawaii, is the most southerly point in the entire USA. It is also home to America's largest free-range Mouflon Sheep herds. South Point has the exclusive hunting rights for this 180-square-mile pristine wilderness. A 4 day hunt, 2x1, costs $2500 per person and includes guide service, transportation from Kona, all meals and soft drinks, packing and skinning of trophy animals, trophy care in the field, and boxing. Not included are trophy fees, hotel accommodations prior to or after the hunt, taxidermy, and shipping fees to taxidermist. Contact Eugene Yap, Professional Hunter.

Phone: 808-322-3201

Fax: 808-322-3630

safaris@gte.net

IDAHO

BARKER TROPHY HUNTS (H)
Idaho, Oregon, Washington
Sheep/Deer/Elk

100% success for 20 years! Deluxe hunts with 2 guides per hunter. Extensive scouting before you arrive. Contact us for recommendations on the best units to apply in. Member, Idaho Outfitters & Guides Association. Jon Barker. Rt. 1 Box 28, Peck, ID 83545.

Phone: 208-924-7809

DAVE WILLIAMS GUIDE SERVICE (H)
Carmen, Idaho
Black Bear/Mountain Lion

One of Idaho's favorite outfitters for black bear and mountain lion. Dave runs a small family operation, based at his home with hunting in the nearby Salmon River area. This is a very vast and rugged country which makes for some great hound hunting while riding one of Dave's sure-footed mules. Expect a strenuous, fast-paced hunt with breathtaking views of some of the most remote areas in this country. Also expect a successful hunt when you're hunting with Dave. Dave's a member of the North American Hunting Club. Box 8, Carmen, ID 83462.

Phone: 208-756-2018.

IDAHO WILDERNESS COMPANY HUNTING & FISHING (H&F)
Central Idaho
Elk/Mule Deer/Bighorn Sheep/Black Bear/Mountain Lion/Moose/Native Cutthroat Trout/Rainbows

Providing Idaho's finest wilderness excursions. Guided big game hunting and fishing in Idaho's Frank Church River of No Return Wilderness. Horseback hunts for elk, mule deer, bighorn sheep, black bear, mountain lion, and moose. Exceptional wilderness stream and lake fishing for native cutthroat and rainbow trout. We offer comfortable wall tent camps, excellent meals, professional guides, and 21 years experience. Owned and operated by Steve and Michelle Zettel.

Phone: 208-879-4700
info@floatidaho.com
www.floatidaho.com

IDAHO WILDERNESS COMPANY RAFT/FISHING TRIPS (F)
Central Idaho
Native Cutthroat Trout/Rainbows

Providing Idaho's finest wilderness excursions. Guided wilderness float trips on the Middle Fork of the Salmon River in Idaho's River of No Return Wilderness. Natural hot springs, gourmet food, beautiful scenery, white water and more enhance the finest 100 miles of native cutthroat and rainbow trout fishing. Our amenities allow for guests of all ages and physical abilities to participate in this unique vacation. Owned and operated by Steve and Michelle Zettel.

Phone: 208-879-4700
info@floatidaho.com
www.floatidaho.com

MYSTIC SADDLE RANCH (H&F)
Stanley, Idaho
*Elk/Mule Deer/Rainbow Trout/
Cutthroats*

Mystic Saddle Ranch has been offering quality wilderness experiences since 1969. We offer a variety of summer family and fishing vacations in the Sawtooth Wilderness as well as a range of fall hunting options. Both our archery and rifle draw bull elk hunts are in a unit that the Idaho Dept. of Fish and Game has listed as having one of the highest bull-to-cow ratios in the state. This means you can hunt for mature bulls in a challenging mountainous setting. Over 50% of the archery hunters who join us for a hunt have taken shots at some of these great trophy animals.

Toll free: 888-722-5432
info@mysticsaddleranch.com
www.mysticsaddleranch.com

TOM LODER'S PANHANDLE OUTFITTERS (H&F)
Northern Idaho
Elk/Deer/Bear/Cougar/Trout

Orvis-endorsed fly fishing in Idaho, Montana and Washington. Full-time outfitter with 27 years professional experience. Trophy elk, deer, bear and mountain lion in North Idaho Panhandle Units 6 and 7, St. Joe River drainage. Archery (Sept.), Rifle (Oct.), Muzzleloader (Nov.), Spring Bear (Apr.–Jun.), Mt. Lion (Dec.–Feb.). Fly fishing on famous Rocky Mountain Rivers including Idaho's St. Joe and

Clearwater, Montana's Clark Fork and Kootenai, and Washington's Spokane and Snake. 12601 S. Thunder Mountain, Valleyford, WA 99036.

Phone: 888-300-HUNT (4868)
panhandle-outfitters@usa.net
www.panhandle-outfitters.com

UNITED STATES OUTFITTERS, IDAHO (H)
Idaho
Sheep/Moose/Mountain Goat

USO has built a tremendous reputation in the hunting industry by hunting the best areas of the Rockies. By guaranteed private land tags as well as draw tags, USO's clients harvest more trophy-class animals than any other outfitter in the nation each year. Archery, muzzleloader, and rifle hunts available. USO handles all the applications through their "professional licensing service" and fronts much of the license cost to their hunters in order to apply to multiple quality areas to have the best chance of obtaining a real trophy hunt. Very comfortable accommodations, great food. Hunt costs are $3450.

Phone: 800-845-9929
www.huntuso.com

VELVET ELK RANCH (H)
Rexburg, Idaho
Trophy Elk

Hunt the majestic bull elk in magnificent, all-natural surroundings. Located just 7 miles from Yellowstone National Park, where you are *guaranteed* a 6x6 or bigger Bull Elk. This is a private ranch with all new individual cabins, great meals, and more elk roaming here than you ever dreamed possible. One-on-one guide. No license required. Gratuities not included in package prices.

Phone: 208-356-0657
harold@yellowstonebearworld.com

WAPITI MEADOW RANCH (F)
Cascade, Idaho
Cutthroat/Rainbow/Bull Trout

A luxury Orvis-endorsed fly fishing lodge featuring remote, people-free streams and high mountain lakes with cutthroat, rainbow and bull trout. Gourmet cuisine and a full-service guest ranch with guided horseback riding, hiking, and fly-out fishing to the wilderness Middle Fork of the Salmon River (July, Aug., Sept. only). 6N/6D Packages from $1500 per person (self-guided) to $2500 per person (fully guided with fly-out). License, taxes and gratuities not included. Contact Diana Bryant.

Tel: 208-633-3217
Fax: 208-633-3219
wapitiMR@aol.com
www.wapitimeadowranch.com

WESTERN WINGS, BIRDS & CLAYS (H)
Idaho Snake River Valley
Upland Birds and Waterfowl Hunts

Western Wings is a 2800-acre membership hunting club with a few openings available to the general public. Located between the Market Lake Wildlife management area to the east and the BLM to the west, Western Wings offers seclusion and privacy while still being easily accessible. Farming practices revolve around the birds and the birds' needs. Dogs and guides are available or you may be your own guide. Basic packages available starting at $180 with no extra accommodations to all-inclusive packages ranging from $1000 to $3500. Contact Dave Robison.

Phone: 208-228-2581
Fax: 208-228-6931
western@birdsandclays.com
www.birdsandclays.com

WORLD CLASS OUTFITTING ADVENTURES (H&F)
Idaho's Selway Bitterroot Wilderness Unit 17
Elk/Mule Deer/Whitetail/Black Bear/ Mountain Lion/Native West Slope Cutthroat/Rainbow Trout

Remote pack-in hunting in the legendary Selway Bitterroot Wilderness area, September–November, rifle season for all species. 2 bears per hunter April–June, bait, hounds, spot & stalk. 2 lions per hunter November–March. Bobcat harvest January and February. Drop camps and fully guided hunts available. Fly packages on the Wild and Scenic Selway River from our Paradise base camp. Cabins starting at $595/person, based on 4-person occupancy. Native West Slope cutthroat and rainbow trout. High mountain lake summer pack trips for the whole family. Call for a free brochure.

Phone: 800-203-3246
www.packin.com

ILLINOIS

SHUDWELL WILDFOWL SPECIALISTS (H)
Southern Illinois
Dove/Canada Goose

Exceptional dove hunting over sunflowers on one of Illinois' premiere dove hunting clubs. Day hunts, afternoons only, $250/person per day. Canada goose hunting on the world-famous Southern Illinois wintering grounds with world champion callers over thousands of decoys. $250/person per day. Mike Weller.

Phone: 217-368-3016

mlwoodduck@yahoo.com

IOWA

SUNDOWN LAKE RECREATIONAL AREA (F)
Moravia, Iowa

Walleye/Largemouth Bass/Crappie

Privately owned 450-acre lake. Fish for walleye, largemouth bass, crappie and more. Celebrity bass tournaments. Live concerts by Nashville artists. Bluegrass festivals. RV sites or stay in our cabins. Shower house, swimming pool and dump station. So peaceful. you may never leave! Contact Bill and Donna Shoop. Home of J&S Trophy Hunts Iowa Camp. See our listing under Missouri.

Phone: 641-724-9276

sundownia@lisco.com

KANSAS

NICKELS FARMS AND OLD SCHOOL GUIDE SERVICE (H&F)
McLouth, Kansas

Whitetail Deer/Quail/Crappie/Bass

Old School Guide Service provides experienced and safety-minded state-licensed commercial guides, dedicated to safe, enjoyable, and successful outings. We offer a limited number of 3- or 5-day guided whitetail deer hunts. Included in the package is transportation to and from Kansas City (Missouri) airport, meals and lodging at the Circle S Ranch. 5-day hunt packages: bow, $2650; firearms, $2950. An additional trophy fee of $600 for any hunt. A Nonresident Deer Permit and Kansas Hunting License are required. Full-day packages are available for wild quail hunting from November through January. We specialize in packages for corporate trips and business travelers.

Phone: 785-863-3465

nickelsfarms@ruralnet1.com

www.oldschoolguideservice.com

RINGNECK RANCH (H)
Tipton, Kansas

Pheasant/Quail/Prairie Chicken

Ringneck Ranch, located in north central Kansas on the Houghtons' fifth-generation homestead, is owned and managed by Keith and Debra Houghton. The hunting operation covers roughly 10,000 acres of the finest pheasant, quail, and prairie chicken habitat. Unusual for most Midwestern wingshooting establishments, accommodations are amid the gunning grounds, with opportunities for every size and type of group. Guests enjoy the ranch's legendary country gourmet cuisine. A full-service hunt package is $335/hunter/day on weekdays and $375/hunter/day weekend. Prices are based on a minimum of 4 hunters per group, with a supplement for smaller parties. For information contact: HC 61 Box 7 Tipton, KS 67485.

Phone: 785-373-4835
ringneck@WTCiweb.com
www.ringneckranch.net

UNITED STATES OUTFITTERS, KANSAS (H)
Kansas
Mule Deer/Whitetail Deer/Pheasant

USO has built a tremendous reputation in the hunting industry by hunting the best areas. By guaranteed private land tags as well as draw tags, USO's clients harvest more trophy-class animals than any other outfitter in the nation each year. Archery, muzzleloader, and rifle hunts available. USO handles all the applications through their "professional licensing service" and fronts much of the license cost to their hunters in order to apply to multiple quality areas to have the best chance of obtaining a real trophy hunt. Very comfortable accommodations, great food. Normally no horseback required. Hunt costs are $3450 with private land tags additional in some areas.

Phone: 800-845-9929
www.huntuso.com

KENTUCKY

STRIPER MADNESS (F)
Russel Springs, Kentucky
Stripers/Rainbows/Browns

Fish one of the nations top striper lakes. Great opportunity to catch a trophy striper, with the average fish weighing 8 to 10 lbs. Each charter is an 8-hour trip unless your limit is caught before that. We will clean and package your catch at no extra cost. Cumberland River trout fishing. All trips from mid-June through September. Each trip will be a float trip down the beautiful and scenic Cumberland River in which live bait, fly fishing, and/or ultra light tackle may be used. Rates: $200 for 2 people, $75 for third person. Ask for packages including lodging and meals.

Phone: 270-866-3660

LOUISIANA

BOURGEOIS CHARTERS (F)
New Orleans, Louisiana
Redfish/Speckled Trout/Black Drum

A Bayou Blast! Fish the beautiful bayou of southern Louisiana for tailing redfish. We are located just 30 minutes from downtown New Orleans! We offer year-round fly and light-tackle fishing. We are the only Orvis-endorsed fishing expedition in Louisiana. Our captains were born and raised on the bayou and know these waters like the back of their hands. Our cabin sleeps up to 16 people. We offer day trips and overnight packages complete with your own private Cajun chef. Give us a call for your trip of a lifetime.

Phone: 504-341-5614
www.neworleansfishing.com

MAINE

LIBBY WILDERNESS LODGE & OUTFITTERS (H)
Ashland, Maine
Black Bear

Maine's wilderness hunting at its best, with proximity to Maine's largest wilderness parks. Big game records. Black bear up to 600 lbs. A hunter's paradise. 6D/6N Packages available. Matt & Ellen Libby.

Phone: 207-435-8274
Fax: 207-435-3230
matt@libbycamps.com

MARYLAND

CAPTAIN BO TOEPFER'S SALTWATER FLY FISHING GUIDE SERVICE (H&F)
Prince Frederick, Maryland
Sea Trout/Speckled Trout/Striped Bass/ Flounder/Cobia/Bluefish/Tuna/Duck/ Goose

Experience some of the finest saltwater fly and light-tackle angling Mother Nature has to offer. We fish Chesapeake Bay, her tributaries and the mid-Atlantic coast. Striped bass is our number one targeted species; you may encounter trout, bluefish, flounder, puppy drum cobia, false albacore and croaker, to name a few. Enjoy fishing flats, marshes and channels. All tackle is provided, but feel free to bring yours if you wish. My lifetime experience is at your service. I welcome the opportunity to share this beautiful area with you. Please bring soft-soled shoes (boat shoes), sunglasses and personal effects; do not forget your camera! Daily rate is $450. Deposit required. For reservations contact: Capt. Bo Toepfer, 1410 Foxtail Lane, Prince Frederick, MD 20678.

Phone: 800-303-4950

MASSACHUSETTS

REEL DREAM CHARTERS (F)
Scituate, Massachusetts

Striped Bass/Bluefish

You will experience world-class striped bass and bluefish action on quality fly and light spinning tackle. We will fish the waters surrounding the historic Boston Harbor Islands, from Hingham to Dorchester Bay, including the Inner Harbor and the islands of the Outer Harbor. Anglers will experience the beauty and challenge of fishing the rocky shoreline of the Outer Harbor Islands to the unique "urban fishing" setting of the Inner Harbor. You'll fish comfortably from a Jones Brothers Cape Fisherman 20-foot Lite Tackle Edition, the "ultimate big water fly and light-tackle craft." Your captain is an Orvis-endorsed Fly-Fishing Guide. The season runs from mid-May to October.

Phone: 781-545-6263
reeldream2@mediaone.com
www.reeldreamcharters.com

MICHIGAN

HAWKINS OUTFITTERS (F)
Traverse City, Michigan
Trout/Steelhead/Salmon

We provide quality guided fly fishing in northwest Lower Michigan year round. From September 15 until May we pursue steelhead in the Manistee and Pere Marquette Rivers. During the summer months we chase browns, brook and rainbow trout. Late August through October 15 Chinook salmon provide tremendous sport. Hawkins Outfitters is an Orvis-endorsed Guide and a FFF-certified Fly Casting Instructor. All skill levels and children welcome. Our rates are $175 to $325 a day depending on number of anglers, length or trip and time of year.

chawkins@traverse.com.
www.hawkinsoutfitters.net

MINNESOTA

CANADIAN WATERS (F)
Ely, Minnesota
Walleye/Northern Pike/Smallmouth Bass
Paddle and fly-in canoe trips into Minnesota's Boundary Waters Canoe Area Wilderness and Ontario's Quetico Provincial Park. Completely outfitted 7-day paddle trips as low as $399 per person. Completely outfitted 7-day round-trip fly-in canoe trips only $850 per person. "North America's only world-class canoe trip outfitter." Visit us on the web or call for our award-winning Packsack Brochure. Dan Waters.

Phone: 800-255-2922
cwmail@canadianwaters.com
www.canadianwaters.com

INTERNATIONAL ANGLING ADVENTURES (F)
International Falls, Minnesota
Smallmouth Bass/Walleye/Northern Pike/Lake Sturgeon/Muskellunge
Come fish these exciting border waters between northern Minnesota and Ontario, Canada, with one of our professional guides. This is the gateway to Voyageur's National Park and the famous Boundary Waters Wilderness Area. These are world-class waters for the species of fish that we will be targeting, including the elusive Muskellunge. Considered by many professional anglers to be the best mixed-bag fishery on earth. So, come take advantage of the fantastic fishing, but remember to enjoy the scenic boat ride and keep an eye out for the abundant wildlife. We can pick you up at the nearby full-service airport and you can choose to stay at one of the area's luxurious lodges, rustic cabins, or quiet campsites or rent a houseboat. A full day of fishing for 2 people is $250 and you will be using the best equipment on the market (and some equipment not yet in the hands of the public).

Toll free: 877-246-7762
bigfish@northwinds.net
www.rainylakefishing.com

NORTH COUNTRY CANOE OUTFITTERS (F)
Ely, Minnesota
Walleye/Northern Pike/ Smallmouth Bass
Completely outfitted wilderness canoe trips through the Boundary Waters Canoe Area Wilderness and Quetico Provincial Park from Ely, Minnesota. Season May to September. 6-day fly-in/fly-out canoe trip into Quetico Park. Pre- and post-trip overnight accommodations included. Licenses and taxes additional. Minimum 2 participants. $700 per person. John Schiefelbein.

Phone: 800-552-5581
john@boundarywaters.com
www.boundarywaters.com

TIMBER TRAIL LODGE (F)
Ely, Minnesota
Walleye/Smallmouth Bass/ Northern Pike
Timber Trail is a wilderness resort with fine lakeside cabins and fully

outfitted Boundary Waters Canoe trips. Northern Minnesota is for those who want to get away from congested heavily fished lakes and get back to the basics. With four lakes available right from your dock and over 600 lakes in the area, your wilderness experience is ready and waiting. Cabins are rented from Saturday to Saturday. There are spring and fall specials for both resort and canoe trips. Call for details.

Phone: 800-777-7348

MISSOURI

ALTENHOF INN BED & BREAKFAST (H&F)
Branson, Missouri
Wild Turkey/Bass

The Ozark Mountains area offers some of the best wild turkey hunting in America. You'll stay at a clean, comfortable bed & breakfast with a beautiful panoramic view of the mountains and Table Rock Lake. 3D/3N package: $410 per two people, double occupancy. Guided fishing and turkey hunting packages extra. Gertrude Santo.

Phone: 417-338-5091
www.altenhofinn.nu

ANGLERS & ARCHERY OUTFITTERS (F)
Branson, Missouri
Trophy Rainbows/Giant Browns

Trophy trout fishing on beautiful Lake Taneycomo and the surrounding White River system. We offer day and night guided trips for trophy rainbows and giant brown trout on any of the White River system's leg-endary tailgaters, with some of the areas most experienced guides. Located just seconds from sections of Lake Taneycomo where you can wade-fish, we offer fine equipment sales/rentals as well as locally tied flies. Whether you're a beginner or experienced, we can customize a trip to fit your needs. Call for reasonable rates or information.

Phone: 417-335-4655
fishcon@tri-lakes.net
www.anglersandarchery.com

BIG CEDAR LODGE (F)
Ridgeview, Missouri
Bass/Trophy Rainbow Trout

Big Cedar Lodge, the Ozarks' premiere wilderness resort, has been touted as "the best of the best" by the *Wall Street Journal*. Located on Table Rock Lake, recognized as one of the top 10 bass fishing lakes in the country. For the reel fisherman, try fly fishing for trophy trout at Dogwood Canyon Nature Park, a 10,000-acre private wilderness refuge, just 20 minutes from the lodge. Package: 3 nights for 2 people in a private log cabin with Jacuzzi, wood-burning fireplace, balcony and kitchen. Includes 2 days bass fishing with guide and 1 day trout fishing with guide. $1772. Taxes, gratuities and license not included.

Phone: 417-335-2777
Fax: 417-335-2340
www.bigcedarlodge.com

BUSTER'S GUIDE SERVICE (F)
Rockaway Beach, Missouri
Bass/Trout/Crappie/Walleye

Enjoy fishing for a variety of species in the beautiful Tri-Lakes area with a professional guide. Table Rock Lake is renowned for its excellent largemouth, smallmouth and spotted bass fishing, any time of the year. Just below the dam is Lake Taneycomo, one of the top five rainbow and brown trout fisheries in the world. Below Taneycomo you will find Bull Shoals, offering great bass, crappie, white bass, and some of the best trophy walleye fishing anywhere. We cater to both the novice and expert fisherman, and would be happy to make group arrangements. A variety of luxury accommodations is available in Branson, just a few miles away from Table Rock, Lake Taneycomo, and Bull Shoals. Coast Guard licensed and insured.

Phone: 417-335-0357
bustersguideservice@inter-linc.net

EXECUTIVE GUIDE SERVICE (F)
Bull Shoals Lake, Missouri
Largemouth/Smallmouth/Kentucky/ White Bass/Crappie

Accommodations, food, guide, gas and tackle are included in package. Rods and reels furnished or you can bring your own. You must provide your own rain gear. Fish the beautiful, clear, peaceful waters of Bull Shoals with Tony Allbright and his professional guides. We offer 3D/3N Packages for two people. Licenses, tax and gratuity not included.

Phone: 800-633-7920, 417-679-4169
Fax: 417-679-3543
pntacldg@webound.com

GARY MARTIN'S PINEY CREEK GUIDE SERVICE (H&F)
Ridgedale, Missouri
Largemouth Bass/Smallmouth/ Kentucky/Rainbow Trout/Browns/ Walleye/Turkey

Come to the heart of the beautiful Ozark Mountains. Fish Table Rock Lake, one of America's great bass lakes, and Lake Taneycomo, one of the best trout lakes in the country. Fish beautiful Bull Shoals Lake for walleye. Catch walleye and trophy bass at night. Gary Martin is Coast Guard licensed and insured, with 25 years experience. Full 8-hour days: $250. 4-hour half-days: $165. Can accommodate up to 3 anglers. Lodging and meals available. Also spring and fall turkey hunts. Contact Gary at: 538 Lindell Drive, Ridgedale, MO 65739.

Phone: 417-239-4221, 417-239-4237
fishtablerock@aol.com

GONE FISHIN' & CO. (F)
Branson, Missouri
Largemouth/Smallmouth/Spotted Bass/White Bass/Rainbow Trout/ Brown Trout/Walleye/Crappie

Over 28 years' experience fishing the area lakes: Taneycomo, Table Rock, Bull Shoals. Full-day and half-day trips. Beginners, corporate groups, and tournament fishermen welcome. Fish from late-model, fully rigged bass boats. Guide fee includes gas, tackle, bait, rod and reels. Full day (8 hrs.) $245, 1 or 2 persons. Half day (4 hrs.) $170, 1 or 2 persons. 3rd person $75.00 extra. Contact Tim Sainato.

Phone: 417-334-8113, 417-335-0037
gofish@inter-linc.net

HAWK I HUNTS (H)
Romance, Missouri
Whitetail Deer/Trophy Turkey

World-record Eastern Wild Turkey have been taken from this area, offering 1200 acres of private land, bordered by Caney Mountain Game Refuge and 1300 acres of additional walk-in public hunting. Packages are $850 for deer, $400 for turkey, per person. We cater to couples. Guides are available at your discretion. These are your hunts! Food and lodging included. You furnish transportation. 4-Wheelers are invited. Ask about our Georgia Wild Hog Hunts.

Phone: 800-422-1321, 417-538-2877

HEARTLAND WILDLIFE RANCHES (H)
Ethel, Missouri
Whitetail/Elk/Red Stag/Exotics/ Turkey

Heartland Wildlife Ranches encompasses 6000 acres of prime hunting habitat in north-central Missouri. With well-managed harvests and breeding of top-quality trophies, you will only be hunting the best of the best. Hunting here means you will be one of 4–6 hunters with 1 on 1 guiding. We pride ourselves in offering very personal and intimate hunting experiences and high-scoring trophies. Accommodations are in our beautiful lodge and include hearty meals boasting the best of the traditional tastes of Midwestern home-style cooking. If you are looking for a fantastic experience call us. Nonhunting companions welcome.

Phone: 888-590-4868
www.heartland-wildlife.com

HOOK'S GUIDE SERVICE (F)
Branson, Missouri
Largemouth/Smallmouth/Spotted Bass

Located just minutes from Branson, Missouri, Table Rock Lake offers some of the best bass fishing in America 12 months of the year. From novice to experienced anglers. Fish with the very best of equipment. Night trips available. Gift certificates available for your favorite angler. Coast Guard licensed, insured. Half day $175, full day $245, 3rd person $50–$75. Winter Special, 6 hours, $175. Bed & breakfast packages available. Contact Jim Van Hook.

Phone: 800-603-4665, 417-338-2277
hooksbass@aol.com
www.hooksbass.com

J&S TROPHY HUNTS (H)
Memphis, Missouri
Trophy Whitetail Deer/ Eastern Turkey

Hunt over 18,000 acres of private land in northern Missouri and southern Iowa with experienced top-notch guides. First-rate lodging. All our packages include guides, meals and lodging. Deer packages: 6-day bow hunt in Iowa, $2000. 6-day bow hunt in Missouri, $1800. 5-day gun hunt in Iowa, $2700. 5-day gun hunt in Missouri, $2600. Turkey Packages: 4-day guided (2 bird), $1000. 3-day guided (1 bird), $750. All you'd expect and more! Now in our 11th year! Full-time outfitter Steve Shoop. Charter member, Iowa Outfitter & Guide's Association. Fully insured. 85% repeat business.

Phone: 660-945-3736
jstrophy@aol.com
www.jstrophyhunts.com

J.B. HUNT'S BIG HORN LODGE (H&F)
Exeter, Missouri
Trout/Elk/Red Stag/Buffalo/Sitka Deer/Axis Deer/Fallow Deer/Texas Dall Sheep/Barbado Sheep/Black Buck Antelope/Turkey/Chukar/Quail/ Pheasant

Nestled in the majestic rolling hills of the Ozarks and surrounded by natural spring-fed mountain streams lies J.B. Hunt's Big Horn Lodge. This exclusive lodge offers five-star quality guest rooms, dining and service. Exotic big game hunting is available for trophy and record species. World-class dogs and experienced guides will assist in the hunting of quail, pheasant and chukar.

Phone: 877-584-4868
www.bighornlodge.com

LAKE OF THE OZARKS MARINA (F)
Camdenton, Missouri
Largemouth Bass/Stripers/Crappie/ Walleye/Muskie/Paddlefish/Sunfish/ Bluegill

Enjoy the ultimate floating fish camp . . . a luxury houseboat rental from Forever Resorts' Lake of the Ozarks Marina! Fish from sunup to sundown without the hassle of a crowded boat ramp—just step off the back deck and into your fishing boat! Each houseboat sleeps 10 in five queen beds and is equipped with all the amenities of home, including gas grill, coffee maker, full-size range, microwave, TV, VCR, central A/C, and 2 refrigerators. We even provide the linens and pots and pans! It's the perfect floating fish camp!

Rates starting at $995 for 4 days/3 nights midweek . . . that's $95 per person for 4 days! North Highway 5, Camdenton, MO 65020.

Phone: 800-255-5561
www.foreverresorts.com/HFD

OTTER CREEK TROPHY RANCH (H)
Deepwater, Missouri
Elk/Whitetail/Turkey

Otter Creek Trophy Ranch covers 2000 acres of prime deer habitat, producing the world's largest trophy animals. Mixture of hardwood and cedar makes hunting very challenging. Last year had two largest bucks taken in Missouri, according to Missouri Archery Big Bucks of MO and one in Show Me Big Bucks. Whitetail and elk hunts begin at $1800. Lodging and meals are included. 100% kill last 10 years. Guide will adapt to your individual hunting needs. Turkey gobblers are also in abundance. Turkey hunts $600. A great experience is waiting for you.

Phone: 417-644-2632

RIVER RUN OUTFITTERS (F)
Branson, Missouri
Brook/Brown/Cutthroat/Rainbow

Lake Taneycomo, part of the White River chain, provides great Rainbow and Brown trout fishing while other parts of the White have Brook and Cutthroat. Guided trips from half- to full-day wade/walk or full-day Western-style drift boat trip while catching trout! Prices range from $95 for 1 person half-day to $250 for 1 or 2 people full-day drift trip. Beginners welcome!

Phone: 877-699-3474, 417-332-0460
shop@riverrunoutfitters.com
www.riverrunoutfitters.com

RUNNING SPRING FARM (H&F)
Everton, Missouri
Upland Birds/Chukar/Pheasant/Bass/
Bluegill/Catfish

Running Spring Farm is an upland bird hunting property for members, their families (spouse or significant other, children 19 or younger at home) and guests. The property is located 35 miles northwest of Springfield, Missouri, isolated by dead-end gravel road to insure seclusion and privacy. Reservations required. Pheasant and chukar partridge year round; quail, rabbit and squirrel in season; fishing and camping; clay target shooting; dog training area; kennels for short-term boarding; clubhouse for small meetings and family gatherings; home-cooked meals; bird cleaning and freezing; guided hunts with our dogs or yours. Yearly membership fees are as follows: Corporate, $8000; Level 2, $4000; Level 1, $1000. Guest fee: $15 per day per guest. To fly in, arrive at Springfield/Branson Regional Airport; transportation available to and from property. Ringneck pheasant hens and roosters: $22.50 each. Chukar partridge: $15 each. Property is under the guidance of a Missouri Department of Conservation Private Lands Biologist to ensure long-term productive habitat for upland birds and wildlife. Bird fields consist of food plots, warm season grasses, briars, wild plum thickets, weeds, brush piles, three half-acre ponds and woodland areas. Contact Bill Cork.

Phone: 417-535-2190
www.billcork.com

SAMMY LANE RESORT (F)
Branson, Missouri
Rainbow/Brown Trout

Come join us for a three-night stay in our clean, spacious, two-bedroom, lakefront cabins. Relax on your own deck overlooking beautiful Lake Taneycomo at "One of *Midwest Living*'s Top 50 Family-Owned Resorts." Package includes two full days of guided drift-boat fly fishing, picked up at your doorstep by River Run Outfitters, on the White River chain. Only $384.99 pp based on double occupancy. Other packages available. 320 East Main Street.

Phone: 417-334-3253
info@sammylaneresort.com
www.sammylaneresort.com

SCOTTY'S GUIDE SERVICE (H)
Springfield, Missouri
Snow Geese/Canadas/Ducks

Some of the best waterfowl hunting in America, located right in the Mississippi flyway. Hunt the wetlands of Stockton Lake, Truman Reservoir, Pomme de Terre, Four Rivers Conservation Area and Schell-Osage. Snow Geese, Canadas, and a variety of species of ducks. $250 for full day of hunting (1x2). Does not include license, guns or shells.

Phone: 417-581-3592
cjoutdoors318365@aol.com

SETTER RIDGE GUN CLUB (H)
Chillicothe, Missouri
Pheasant/Quail/Chukar/Exotics

Hunt among the beautiful rolling hills of northwest Missouri! Our guides can lead you over thousands of acres of native grasslands, up fencerows and through specially conditioned crop land, for the best upland bird hunting around. We offer various hunting packages to fit your schedule. Large groups welcome. Hunts are scheduled from Sept. 1 through April 1. Half-Day Hunt: $150 per hunter, includes 6 quail, 3 pheasant, 4 chukar and one meal. Full-Day Hunt: $275 per hunter. Limit 12 quail, 5 pheasant, and two meals. 1 to 3-Day Hunts with overnight stay: $300 per person per day. No limits on birds. Includes three meals per day, kennel service and mini-sporting clay course.

Phone: 660-772-3166
www.setteridge.com

SHIRATO OUTDOOR ADVENTURES (H&F)
Springfield, Missouri
High-Quality North & South American Destinations for Hunting & Fishing

We unite the hunter and fisherman with quality destinations and experienced guides. Whether you're planning to hunt grizzly bear, stone sheep, caribou, antelope, doves, ducks or geese— or fish for peacock bass, largemouths, smallmouths, pyrarah, northern pike, walleye or the 5 species of salmon, we can customize a trip specifically for your needs. We arrange hunting and fishing trips to Brazil, Venezuela, Mexico, Canada and Alaska.

Phone: 417-869-0727
Fax: 417-869-5234

info@shiratooutdoor.com
www.shiratooutdoor.com

STATE PARK MARINA (F)
Branson, Missouri
Table Rock Lake Fishing

Enjoy a day cruising the beautiful waters of Table Rock Lake and try your luck fishing for warm-water species of fish such as large- and smallmouth bass, spotted bass, catfish and sunfish. Be the captain of an easy-to-operate fishing pontoon or traditional fishing boat. The package for 3 people includes fishing pontoon boat and fuel, fishing rods, one-day fishing licenses, and 3-dozen worms. $299. Professional guided trips also available. Phillip Cox.

Phone: 417-334-2628

TABLE ROCK LAKE-BRANSON HOUSEBOAT RENTALS (F)
Ridgedale, Missouri
Largemouth Bass/Stripers/Crappie/Walleye/Muskie/Paddlefish/Sunfish/Bluegill

Enjoy the ultimate floating fish camp—a luxury houseboat rental from Forever Resorts' Branson Houseboat Rentals! Fish from sunup to sundown without the hassle of a crowded boat ramp—just step off the back deck and into your fishing boat! Each houseboat sleeps 10 in five queen beds and is equipped with all the amenities of home, including gas grill, coffee maker, full-size range, microwave, TV, VCR, central A/C and 2 refrigerators. We even provide the linens and pots and pans! Rates starting at $995 for 4 days/3 nights midweek . . . that's $95 per person for 4 days! 915 Long Creek Road, Ridgedale, MO 65739.

Phone: 800-255-5561

www.foreverresorts.com/HFD

TABLE ROCK LAKE RESORT (F)
Ridgedale, Missouri
Largemouth Bass/Stripers/Crappie/ Walleye/Muskie/Paddlefish/Sunfish/ Bluegill

Just minutes from Branson, Missouri, Table Rock Lake Resort is within walking distance of beautiful Table Rock Lake. With 4 room types available, Table Rock Lake Resort can accommodate a couple or an entire group. Enjoy our two packages: The $350 Fisherman's Dream Package includes 2 nights lodging for two in the Resort, plus two full days of fishing on a new and fully equipped Tracker Bass Boat. Or try the $375 Family Getaway Package that includes 3 nights lodging for four at the Resort, plus one full day on a new Tracker Pontoon Boat. Tax, fuel, deposits and damage waiver are not included. 915 Long Creek Road, Ridgedale, MO 65738.

Phone: 800-877-9235

www.tablerocklakeresort.com/HFD

WHITE RIVER OUTFITTERS (F)
Shell Knob, Missouri, and

Eureka Springs, Arkansas
Brown/Rainbow Trout

Let WRO Guide Service show you some of the finest trout fishing that Missouri and Arkansas have to offer. Whether it be fall night fly-fishing trips for giant brown trout, or family outings with great spincast fishing for beautiful Lake Taneycomo rainbows, WRO is happy to provide all the equipment and water knowledge to make your Ozark visit one you will come back for year after year. Federally licensed and insured, our prestigious sponsors' list guarantees great equipment and trust by some of the biggest names in outdoor sports: Orvis, Evinrude, Ford, Falcon, St. Croix, Berkley, Stratos, ESPN Radio. Full- and half-day trips available. Rates: Full-day Taneycomo $225, White River $250. Half-day Taneycomo $175. Rates are for 1 or 2 people. Extra person $75.00. Everything provided, including resort pickup and return.

Phone: 800-544-0257

WIL-NOR HUNT CLUB (H)
Dittmer, Missouri
Whitetail Deer/Wild Turkey/Upland Birds (Pheasant and Quail)

20,000 acres of prime whitetail deer, turkey and upland bird hunting in northern Missouri. Three-day rifle or archery deer hunt $1250. Two-day turkey hunt $500. Two-day upland bird hunt $600. Experienced guide, top-notch bird dogs, food and lodging included. Insured. Bill Kunz.

Phone: 636-274-4233

www.wil-nor.com

MONTANA

BAGLEY GUIDE SERVICE (H&F)
Bigfork, Montana
Lake Trout/Mountain Lion

Come along on a first-class charter fishing trip on beautiful Flathead Lake. Fishing will be for big lake trout ranging from 5 to 20+ pounds. Top-of-the-line boats and state-of-the-art equipment will allow you to catch "the one that didn't get away." Half-day and full-day trips available. Guaranteed fish! Bagley Guide Service is also considered to be one of the premier Mountain Lion guides in the West. Our reputation speaks for itself, as our success rate on big mature Mountain Lions is 100%.

Phone: 406-837-3618
www.montanaweb.com/hunting

BATTLE CREEK LODGE (F)
Choteau, Montana
Kamloops Rainbow Trout/West Slope Cutthroat/German Brown/Brook

Located 32 miles southwest of Choteau, Montana, Battle Creek Lodge is at the very foot of the towering Rocky Mountains. The lodge and our two private cabins have provided secluded getaways for over 10 years. With a maximum occupancy of 12 guests, our lodge offers incredible fishing and an intimate, relaxing setting. In our 8 spring-fed lakes, you will find trophy trout that will challenge the most accomplished fly fisher, while at the same time are forgiving to those among us who perhaps have never fly-fished. Our Kamloops Rainbow have been recorded as large as 31 inches, weighting 15 pounds.

The average size is an equally impressive 19 inches, weighing 2 to 3 pounds. Sample packages: 5 days, 4 nights, $1795 pp/dbl occp; 6 days, 5 nights, $1995 pp/dbl occp; 7 days, 6 nights, $2295 pp/dbl occp. If you are looking for trophy fish, good food, relaxation and solitude, give us a call. Contact Jack Salmond.

Phone: 406-466-2815, 406-799-0499
www.battlecreeklodge.com

BEAVER CREEK OUTFITTERS (H)
Central Montana
Elk/Mule Deer/Summer Vacation Trips

We offer excellent hunting opportunities for both mule deer and elk in the National Forest. Our guided bow hunts are either 7 or 10 days. Our guided rifle hunts are 7 days. Our fully outfitted tent camp is located in the Little Belt Mountains and is reached by a 2-hour pack trip. Horses are used extensively. We offer summer vacation trips—either at our mountain camp or progressive trips—customized to meet your needs. 7- and 10-day archery hunts, $1200–$1700. 7-day guided (2 on 1) combination rifle/archery hunts, $2500. Insured, #3746. Approved by NAHC; Member, Montana Outfitters & Guides, and Rocky Mountain Elk Foundation.

Phone: 800-355-7557
Fax: 406-538-5706

BIGHORN RIVER RESORT (H&F)
Bighorn River, Montana
Rainbow/Brown/Cutthroat/Brook/Golden Trout/Duck

Cast and blast! Fly fish and hunt ducks on the Bighorn, a magical tailwater known for prolific year-round hatches and gin-clear water. Rainbows and browns. Hand-crafted log lodge and deluxe guest cabins. Gourmet cooking. 4D/5N lodging, fishing and waterfowl hunting: $2300 per person, double occupancy.

Phone: 800-665-3799
info@forrestersbighorn.com
www.forrestersbighorn.com

BIG TIMBER GUIDES (H&F)
Big Timber, Montana
Elk/Mule Deer/Whitetail/Mountain Lion/Antelope/Black Bear/Mountain Goat/Moose/Big Horn Sheep/ Rainbow Trout/Browns/Cutthroat

Welcome to Montana! The area where we hunt Elk, Deer and Moose is in the Gallatin National Forest, between the Yellowstone River and the Absaroka/Beartooth Wilderness area, just north of Yellowstone Park. Having hunted and guided this area for over 20 years, I feel I am an expert in the guide business and can offer you some of the best hunting in Montana. We offer a wide variety of hunting and fishing services to meet your specific needs. Elk-Deer 5-day Combination Hunts start at $2800. Fly fishing trips start at $300 daily. 4-Day Wilderness Pack trips start at $1000. Contact Bob Bovee.

Phone: 406-932-4080

CIRCLE KBL OUTFITTERS & GUIDES (H&F)
Darby, Montana
Elk/Whitetails/Mulies/Black Bear/ Mountain Lion/Native Cutthroat Trout

Montana's premier outfitter for elk, deer, bear and lion. Horse pack-in or stay in our modern lodge. Guided, semi-guided or drop camps. Private and public land, trophy elk management area. Affordable rates. Gentle horses. Guaranteed licenses. Experienced guides. Bugle season bowhunts. Quality equipment. Combo hunts. Summer wilderness pack trips. Remote solitude. Member, Rocky Mountain Elk Foundation. Contact Scott Boulanger.

Phone: 406-821-0017
Fax: 406-821-3589
elkhunter@montana.com
www.circlekbl.com

DIAMOND J RANCH (H&F)
Ennis, Montana
Rainbow/Brown/Brook Trout/ Pheasant/Hungarian Partridge/ Chukars

An Orvis-endorsed fishing and wingshooting lodge, elevation 5800 feet, surrounded by the Lee Metcalf Wilderness. Capacity 30–35. Fish Jack Creek alongside of the ranch, 14 different lakes, or the Madison River just 12 miles away. There's also horseback riding, hiking, bird watching, or just plain relaxing. We have a babysitter (July and August), kids' dining room. No TV or phones in the rustic log cabins. Each cabin has its own fireplace, private bath and front porch. No smog, and a view that is out of sight.

Phone: 877-929-4867 (Tim Combs),
    877-658-5291 (Luke Eidt, Wing
    Shooting Manager)
www.ranchweb.com/diamondj

THE DIVIDE WILDERNESS RANCH (H)
Southwestern Montana
Elk/Mule Deer/Black Bear

The wilderness surrounding the The Divide Wilderness Ranch is home to a variety of wildlife, including elk, deer, moose, antelope, bear, coyote, wolves, cougar, and over 200 species of birds. We offer quality, fair chase rifle and archery hunts in some of the most beautiful country Montana has to offer. Either hunt from base camp at the ranch or pack into and hunt from one of our many high-country wilderness camps in the Centennial and Tendoy Mountain ranges. And unlike other outfitters, our packers will pack the gear in and out, allowing our guests more time to hunt. Archery Elk/Deer Combo (2 on 1) 6-day hunt, $2300. Rifle Elk/Deer Combo (2 on 1) 6-day hunt, $2850. We are member of the Rocky Mountain Elk Foundation.

Toll free: 888-764-3300
info@divideranch.com
www.divideranch.com

FLATHEAD LAKE LODGE (H&F)
Bigfork, Montana
Rainbow/Cutthroat/Northern Pike/ Lake Trout/Largemouth Bass

Located near Glacier National Park and Bob Marshall Wilderness. Weekly vacations featuring extensive outdoor recreation: horseback riding, fly fishing, river floats, lake and stream fishing, sailing, tennis, cookouts, mountain biking and more. Operated since 1945 by the Averill family. Received numerous accolades for best Western vacation in Montana and the U.S. The lodge also operates a full fishing, rafting and hunting service. It features a game preserve with elk, bison and mountain goats. An all-inclusive 7-day package vacation is $2186 adult, less for children.

Phone: 406-837-4391
Fax: 406-837-6977
fll@digisys.net
www.averills.com

FLAT IRON OUTFITTING (H&F)
Thompson Falls, Montana
Whitetail/Elk/Mule Deer/Lion/Bear/ Fishing

We specialize in whitetail deer on our 2400 acre private ranch lease. Elk are taken on the ranch every year. The lease borders the Lolo National Forest. Most elk, bear and mountain lion hunts are on National Forest land. High mountain lakes provide excellent fishing for cutthroat and brook trout. Bank fishing from the river for perch, pike, bass, browns, and rainbow trout. Lic. # 2435. NAHC approved.

Phone: 406-827-3666
flatiron@blackfoot.net

HAWLEY MOUNTAIN OUTFITTERS (H)
McLeod, Montana
Elk/Whitetail/Mulies

Hunting in the Absaroka Beartooth Wilderness north of Yellowstone Park. Good mature bulls in rugged mountain terrain. Mule deer also available, but we usually concentrate on elk. Accommodations in our guest ranch lodge or a tent camp 7 miles in. 6 days guided (2 on 1), $350 per person per day.

Other packages available. Lic. #507. Ron Jarrett.

Toll free: 877-496-7848
jarrett.ronald@mcleodusa.net

MARK YOUNG'S HUNTING SERVICES (H&F)
Augusta, Montana
Rainbow/Brown/Kamloop Hybrids/ Elk/Whitetail/Pheasant/Sharptail/ Ducks/Geese

We specialize in large whitetail on 30,000 acres of private land. Excellent archery hunting in September and November. 10 miles of river bottom for fishing.

Phone: 406-562-3250

MONTANA HIGH COUNTRY TOURS (H&F)
Southwest Montana
Big Game/Trout/Snowmobiling

Year-round guide service to Montana's best hunting, fishing, horseback and snowmobiling. Experienced professional guides, new spacious lodge, delicious family-style meals. Established in 1979. Trophy possibilities for both hunting and trout fishing. Hunting trips from $300 per day, trout fishing trips from $175 per day, and snowmobiling trips from $125 per day.

Phone: 406-683-4920
montana@mhct.com
www.mhct.com

MONTANA SAFARIS (H&F)
Bob Marshall and Scapegoat Wilderness, Montana
Elk/Mule Deer/Black Bear/Mountain Lion/Summer Horseback, Fishing and Photography

Montana's most authentic adventures, our hunting safaris will take you into untamed wilderness in search of trophy elk, deer, bear, or mountain lion. 8- and 9-day hunts are conducted with two hunters per guide, $2500 to $3200, respectively. Our summer progressive pack trips create precious memories for both groups or individuals. With panoramic views of alpine peaks and high mountain meadows and scratch-cooked camp cuisine, our summer trips are sure to please. Summer rates are $175 per person per day. Family owned and operated. Rocky and Lorell Heckman.

Phone: 406-466-2004
safaris@3rivers.net
www.montanasafaris.simplenet.com

MOUNTAIN LAKE FISHERIES (F)
Northwest Montana Rockies
Whitefish/Cutthroat/Rainbow/Bull/ Lake Trout

Let our experienced guides show some of the hottest fall fishing on northwest Montana's Flathead River. Located near Glacier National Park, the fall and early winter mountain scenery is spectacular! From our heated 18-foot jet boat, you'll startle whitetail deer, jump flocks of Canadian honkers, watch eagles soar over quiet river pools, and listen to the occasional cackling of rooster pheasants . . . all on the same day! Catch up to 50 scrappy 2 lb. or bigger lake whitefish per day on light spinning tackle. Although we concentrate on whitefish, you may also catch occasional cutthroat, rainbow, bull, and lake trout.

Phone: 888-809-0826
mtlkfish@whitefishcaviar.com
www.whitefishcaviar.com

PIONEER OUTFITTER (H&F)
Wise River, Montana
Cutthroat/Rainbow/Brown/Brook/
Grayling/Elk/Mule Deer/Whitetail/
Black Bear/Mountain Lion/Moose/
Goat/Bighorn Sheep/Antelope

Pioneer Outfitter is a small family-owned and -operated guide service in Southwest Montana's Big Hole Valley. Spring Black Bear, spot and stalk hunts. Fall hunting for trophy-class elk, mule & whitetail deer and mountain lion. Horse pack-in hunts at a comfortable back-country tent camp or base camp hunts. 7-day horseback hunts from $2800. 6-day, 4x4 base camp hunts from $2400. Fish Southwest Montana's finest blue-ribbon streams, the Big Hole and Beaverhead Rivers or horseback day, or, by overnight trips, remote Alpine Lakes. Starting at $300 per day for a party of 2.

Phone: 406-832-3132
pioneeroutfitter@montana.com

SKYLINE GUIDE SERVICE (H&F)
Cooke City, Montana
Elk/Mule Deer/Black Bear/Moose/
Rainbow/Cutthroat/Brook Trout

Here in the heart of outdoor recreation paradise, we just about do it all. We fish some of the best waters in the Rockies and hunt Area 316, which is the early bugling season for either sex of elk. Comfortable accommodations, great food, experienced guides, gentle horses. 7 day (2-on-1) combination

hunts, $2400. Fishing packages from 1 to 7 days. Horseback riding and wilderness camping at its best at affordable prices.

Phone: 877-238-8885
www.elkhuntmontana.com

SPOTTED BEAR RANCH (H&F)
Kalispell, Montana
Cutthroat Trout/Trophy Elk/Deer/
Black Bear

Alpine Adventures at Spotted Bear Ranch is Northwest Montana's Orvis-endorsed Fly Fishing Lodge and Guest Ranch. Located at the end of a 60-mile, unpaved road and right on the bank of the uncrowded South Fork of the Flathead River. Our experienced, professional guides take guests float and wade fly fishing for wild, native Westslope cutthroat trout—on dry flies! The challenging access to our pristine and secluded waters means they're rarely fly-fished. We also take adventurous backcountry pack trips into Montana's largest wilderness area, the 1.5 million-acre Bob Marshall Wilderness Complex. When not fly fishing, we trophy hunt for Rocky Mountain big game—elk, deer and black bear. Our guests enjoy private, modern cabins with fireplaces. All activities—fishing, horseback riding, etc.—are included. 5D/6N Lodge-based Fly Fishing Vacation: $2125/person, double occupancy, all-inclusive, two guests per guide. Contact Fred Haney or Kirk Gentry for other fishing and hunting rates.

Phone: 800-223-4333, 406-755-7337
sbr@montana.com
www.spottedbear.com

UNITED STATES OUTFITTERS, MONTANA (H)
Montana
Sheep/Mountain Goat/Moose

USO has built a tremendous reputation in the hunting industry by hunting the best areas of the Rockies. By guaranteed private land tags as well as draw tags, USO's clients harvest more trophy-class animals than any other outfitter in the nation each year. Archery, muzzleloader, and rifle hunts available. USO handles all the applications through their "professional licensing service" and fronts much of the license cost to their hunters in order to apply to multiple quality areas to have the best chance of obtaining a real trophy hunt. Very comfortable accommodations, great food. Hunt costs are $3450.

Phone: 800-845-9930
www.huntuso.com

WILD TROUT ADVENTURES (F)
Northern Montana Rockies
Cutthroat/Rainbow/Brook/Arctic Grayling/Lake Superior Whitefish

Welcome to Wild Trout Adventures, your source for fly fishing around Glacier National Park. We're located right in the middle of some of North America's finest fly-fishing rivers, with the famous Flathead and Swan Rivers just minutes away. Wild Trout Adventures offers guiding services on these incredible rivers and local mountain lakes. We also have spring fishing for warm-water species. All gear is provided on trips.

Phone: 406-837-3838
wldtrout@digisys.net

WW OUTFITTERS (H)
Darby, Montana
Elk/Mule Deer/Whitetail/Black Bear/ Mountain Lion/Moose/Mountain Goat/Bighorn Sheep

WW Outfitters takes pride in providing our guests with the most successful and memorable Montana big game hunts available. Whether you are after Montana trophy elk, mountain lion, spring black bear, mule deer, whitetail deer, moose, mountain goat or bighorn sheep, our experienced guides will lead you there. We provide the very best in elk hunting, and we have guaranteed hunts available. If it's big game you're after, WW Outfitters can put you in the right area to fill your tag. We're members of the Rocky Mountain Elk Foundation. Contact Jeryl Williams, Owner.

Phone: 406-821-3611
jerylw@montana.com

YELLOWSTONE VALLEY RANCH (F)
Paradise Valley, Montana
Rainbow/Brook/Brown/Cutthroat

A great diversity of water to fish is just minutes, if not steps, from the lodge, including the renowned spring creeks of Paradise Valley, the fabled Yellowstone River, a wide variety of smaller freestone streams, and all the fine rivers in the northern part of Yellowstone National Park. Perched on a bluff overlooking the Yellowstone River, the ranch provides comfortable accommodations and fine cuisine.

Phone: 800-245-1950
www.frontierstrvl.com

NEBRASKA

GREAT PLAINS GUIDE SERVICE (H&F)
Scottsbluff, Nebraska
Trophy Walleye/Bass/Goose

We invite you to come to the scenic Panhandle of Nebraska and enjoy some of the best fishing and hunting in the Midwest. We offer fishing at Lake McConaughy (Nebraska's largest lake) for trophy walleye (5–10 lb. limits common) or Largemouth Bass (75+ in the 2–8 lb. class caught daily), or both—it's up to you. Also fishing for stripers, wipers, and trout. And Canaa Goose hunting at its finest!! Clean, comfortable lodging, first-class meals, and knowledgeable guides make this trip unforgettable. For information on packages or a free brochure, contact Kerry Keane. References available.

Phone: 888-632-1040, 308-631-5160.
kkeane@globalcentral.com

NEVADA

CALLVILLE BAY MARINA (F)
Lake Mead, Nevada
Largemouth Bass/Smallmouth Bass/ Stripers/Crappie/Catfish/Bluegill

Enjoy the ultimate floating fish camp—a luxury houseboat rental from Forever Resorts' Callville Bay Marina! Fish from sunup to sundown without the hassle of a crowded boat ramp—just step off the back deck and into your fishing boat! Each houseboat sleeps 10 in five queen beds and is equipped with all the amenities of home, including gas grill, coffee maker, full-size range, microwave, TV, VCR, central A/C and 2 refrigerators. We even provide the linens and pots and pans! Rates starting at $995 for 4 days/3 nights midweek . . . that's $95 per person for 4 days! HCR-30, Box 100, Las Vegas, NV 89124.

Phone: 800-255-5561
www.foreverresorts.com/HFD

COTTONWOOD COVE MARINA (F)
Lake Mohave, Nevada
Largemouth Bass/Smallmouth Bass/ Stripers/Crappie/Rainbow Trout/ Catfish/Bluegill

Enjoy the ultimate floating fish camp—a luxury houseboat rental on Lake Mohave—home of the 60-lb.+ Stripers—from Forever Resorts' Cottonwood Cove Marina! Fish from sunup to sundown without the hassle of a crowded boat ramp—just step off the back deck and into your fishing boat! Each houseboat sleeps 10 in five queen beds and is equipped with all the amenities of home, including gas grill, coffee maker, full-size range, microwave, TV, VCR, central A/C and 2 refrigerators. We even provide the linens and pots and pans! Rates starting at $995 for 4 days/3 nights midweek . . . that's $95 per person for 4 days! 1000 Cottonwood Cove Road, Cottonwood Cove, NV 89046.

Phone: 800-255-5561
www.foreverresorts.com/HFD

COTTONWOOD RANCH OUTFITTERS (H&F)
Jarbidge Wilderness, Wells, Nevada
*Mule Deer/Elk/Mountain Lion/
Antelope/Rocky Mountain Bighorn
Sheep/Upland Birds/Native Trout*

Premier high-country Northeastern Nevada Jarbidge wilderness hunts. Area 7, O'Neil Basin, Wells, Nevada. Trophy elk, mule deer and mountain lion. Fully guided pack-in hunts and drop camps. Top-notch guides. Rifle, archery, and muzzleloader. Special non-resident outfitter deer tag applications are given around the first of February and are due back around March 10 of each year. Mountain lion tags are sold over the counter. We use top-notch hounds along with horses, snowmobiles and 4x4's to get the job done. We also offer bighorn sheep, antelope and upland hunts; summertime pack trips; fishing; cattle and horse drives; and ranch vacations. The Smith family is a 3-generation working cattle and outfitting ranch. For info and booking information, contact Blain Jackson.

Phone: 208-952-1111
blainjackson@aol.com
www.findoutfitters.com/cottonwood

MUSTANG OUTFITTERS (H&F)
Round Mountain, Nevada
*Trophy Elk/Mule Deer/Mountain
Lion/Desert Bighorn Sheep/Antelope/
Varmint/Chukar/Grouse/Rainbow
Trout/Brooks/Browns*

Wilderness trophy hunts for elk, mule deer, mountain lion, and desert bighorn sheep. Also antelope, varmint and upland game bird hunts. Wilderness trout fishing trips as well as wilderness pack trips, photo safaris, elk and desert sheep viewing. We also have the 4-day Toiyabe Crest Trail Ride and will customize our pack trips to suite your needs. Most elk, deer, and sheep hunts are on horseback, but we do offer 4x4 hunts outside the wilderness areas for mule deer. Member, Rocky Mountain Elk Foundation.

Phone: 775-964-2145
mustangoutfitters@austin.igate.com
mustangoutfitters@hotmail.com
www.huntersmall.com/mustang/mustang.htm

UNITED STATES OUTFITTERS, NEVADA (H)
Nevada
Elk/Mule Deer/Antelope/Sheep

USO has built a tremendous reputation in the hunting industry by hunting the best areas of the Rockies. By guaranteed private land tags as well as draw tags, USO's clients harvest more trophy-class animals than any other outfitter in the nation each year. Archery, muzzleloader, and rifle hunts available. USO handles all the applications through their "professional licensing service" and fronts much of the license cost to their hunters in order to apply to multiple quality areas to have the best chance of obtaining a real trophy hunt. Very comfortable accommodations, great food. Normally no horseback required. Hunt costs are $3450.

Phone: 800-845-9929
www.huntuso.com

NEW MEXICO

CK OUTFITTERS (H)
New Mexico Hunting
Elk/Deer/Antelope/Bear/Lion/Turkey

We are experts in the areas we hunt and the game we seek. Hunting locations are in the National Forest as well as private land throughout the state. We are proud to be one of the first three registered guides in New Mexico. Great accommodations, food and enjoyable hunting experiences. All hunts are 1x1 guided hunts with some combination dates. Chester R. Connor, Jr., and Katie Taylor, outfitters.

Phone: 505-682-5500
www.ckoutfitters.com

COLLINS RANCH (H)
San Jon, New Mexico
Trophy Mule Deer/Whitetail/Wild Turkey

Hunt mule deer and occasional whitetail on 29,000 acres of open ranch. No bait situations. 3-day/3-night hunts. Package hunts: $1500 per person, and lodging, food, and meat preparation. $850 turkey hunts, inclusive. Dolan Hawkins. Other hunts available: Georgia Hogs and more.

Phone: 800-422-1321, 417-538-2877
Web site: www.rockspringsretreat.com

5M OUTFITTERS (H)
Chama, New Mexico
Elk/Mule Deer/Mountain Lion/Bear/Turkey

Specializing in private land elk hunts, with no drawing for license. We also offer outfitting for mountain lion, mule deer, bear, and turkey. All hunts are 5 days. Private land bull elk hunts are $4850. The other hunts have different prices. Call for prices. We are a full-service outfitter and keep the hunters in a lodge. Nonhunting guests are welcome. Outfitter member of Rocky Mountain Elk Foundation. Member, NM Council Outfitter & Guides, Chama Valley Chamber of Commerce, and Chama Valley Search & Rescue.

Phone: 505-588-7003
www.5Moutfitters.com

HORIZON GUIDE & OUTFITTERS (H)
Socorro, New Mexico
Elk/Mule Deer/Coues Deer/Antelope/Black Bear/Cougar

Trophy hunting on premier public and private lands in southwest and south-central New Mexico. Excellent experienced guides. Your success and satisfaction keeps me in business. 5-day rifle elk hunt, $3000. Muzzleloader and archery, $2800. Archery is 6 days. Member, Rocky Mountain Elk Foundation. Kelly Dow.

Phone: 505-835-0813
Fax: 505-835-2238
kelly@horizonoutfitters.com
www.horizonoutfitters.com

RANCHO ROJO OUTFITTING SERVICE (H)
Coyote, New Mexico
Elk/Mule Deer/Antelope

Quality New Mexico big game hunts including elk, mule deer and antelope. Archery, rifle and black powder hunts available for all species.

Hunts are held on a combination of private and public lands. Modern lodging with homemade meals. Hunts are conducted by 4-wheel drive to hunt area and walking in thereafter. Professional, personal and honest service. Airport pickup, trophy and meat care, and 2x1 guide service included on all hunts.

Phone: 505-638-5004

RB OUTFITTER AND GUIDE SERVICES (H&F)
Bosque, New Mexico
Trout/Mule Deer/Elk/Antelope/ Turkey/Varmint

Quality hunting and trout fishing on private, National Forest and wilderness land. We hunt all rifle, muzzleloader and bow seasons. Seasons are from early September through December. Fishing trips are done in summer, June through September, also on private land or wilderness, with horseback trips available. Very fun for the whole family. Our accommodations consist of rustic yet very comfortable tents and cabins. Hunt packages start at: Elk $2500 and up, Mule Deer $2500, Antelope $1500. Varmints and fishing trips $150 per day per person. Lic. #0169. Ron & Blanche Schalla. PO Box 506, Bosque, NM 87006.

Phone: 505-864-2379

SKY HIGH OUTFITTERS (H)
New Mexico
Elk

Trophy bow and muzzleloading big game hunts, south of Acoma Indian Reservation in New Mexico. Hunt 250,000 acres of BLM, wilderness, and National Forest. Comfortable accommodations with two sleeping cabins, and log cabin lodge with fireplace, wet bar and two bathrooms. Archery hunts in September, one on one: $3500.00. October muzzleloading hunts, one on one: $3900.00 (license draw for muzzleloading hunts). Two on one hunts also available. Bonded and insured. Jim Johnson.

Phone: 517-835-6671
Fax: 517-835-7147
donnap@jejohnson.com
www.skyhighoutfitters.com

TALISMAN HUNTING (H)
New Mexico and Texas
Elk/Mule Deer/Antelope/Turkey

We specialize in big game hunting in New Mexico. All hunts are fully guided and outfitted on private land with guaranteed licenses—no draw. Airport pick-up and delivery from Albuquerque. Elk hunts from permanent bunkhouse-style lodge. Antelope and mule deer out of tent camps. Costs range from $1600 (antelopes) to $4750 (elk, rifle) to $2500 (deer, rifle). References available. We also offer big game hunting in Alaska. For more information, call Chuck Berg.

Phone: 800-753-1139

TIMBERLINE OUTFITTERS (H&F)
Luna, New Mexico
Trout/Largemouth/Smallmouth Bass/ Crappie/Sunfish/Catfish/Elk/Mule Deer/Coues Deer/Antelope/Bighorn Sheep/Mountain Lion/Black Bear/ Javelina/Turkey/Duck/Quail/Dove

Hello and thank you for your interest in Timberline Outfitters. My name is Perry Hunsaker. I am a full time outfitter and guide. I provide hunts in New Mexico Arizona, and Mexico. Most hunts are done on a one-on-one basis unless other arrangements are preferred. We provide all meals, lodging and field care of your animals. I believe my guides are the best in the business. They are true professionals! We want your trip to be memorable as well as a rewarding experience. So if you're dreaming of a first class hunt, a trophy class animal and a top rated outfitter, give Timberline Outfitters a call and let's go hunting! Contact us at PO Box 38, Luna, NM 87824.

Phone: 480-988-9654, 505-547-2413
www.timberlineoutfitters.com

UNITED STATES OUTFITTERS NEW MEXICO (H)
New Mexico
*Elk/Mule Deer/Whitetail/Antelope/
Sheep/Moose/Mountain Goat/
Mountain Lion/Black Bear/Pheasant*

USO has built a tremendous reputation in the hunting industry by hunting the best areas of the Rockies. By guaranteed private land tags as well as draw tags, USO's clients harvest more trophy-class animals than any other outfitter in the nation each year. Archery, muzzleloader, and rifle hunts available. USO handles all the applications through their "professional licensing service" and fronts much of the license cost to their hunters in order to apply to multiple quality areas to have the best chance of obtaining a real trophy hunt. Very comfortable accommodations, great food. Normally

no horseback required. Hunt costs are $3450, with private land tags additional in some areas.

Phone: 800-845-9929
www.huntuso.com

UU BAR RANCH (H&F)
Northeastern New Mexico
*Elk/Mule Deer/Antelope/Turkey/
Rainbow/Brown/Brook/Cutthroat*

The UU Bar Ranch, nestled in the beautiful Sangre de Cristo Mountains, is located near Angel Fire, New Mexico. This privately owned, 112,000-acre,175-square-mile ranch offers exceptional hunting and fishing opportunities. All private waters. Trophy elk, antelope and deer hunting. Spring turkey.

Toll free: 877-HUNTFISH
www.westernstatesoutdoors.com

NEW YORK

BEAVER BROOK OUTFITTERS (F)
Adirondack Mountains
Smallmouth Bass/Brook Trout

Fish the pristine Hudson River Gorge and Central Adirondacks for trout and smallmouth bass from late April to Columbus Day. One- to three-day wilderness float trips and full- or half-day wading trips available. Fly or hike in to back-country ponds for native brookies. The Adirondack Park has over 2000 lakes and ponds and thousands of miles of rivers and streams. Come enjoy the largest wilderness area east of the Mississippi. Orvis-endorsed. PO Box 96 Wevertown, NY 12886.

Phone: 888-454-8433
pete@beaverbrook.net
www.beaverbrook.net

FIN CHASER CHARTERS (F)
Staten Island, New York
Striped Bass/Blue/Weakfish/Bonito/
False Albacore/Dorado/Tuna

Come fish the "Big Apple." Fly fish or spin casting in New York Harbor, Raritan Bay, Jamaica Bay, Breezy Point to Sandy Hook. Catch striped bass, blues, weakfish, bonito and false albacore. Offshore trips available for tuna, dorado and sharks. Also Montauk's Fall Blitzs (Sept. and Oct.). Manhattan pick-ups can be arranged. Inshore 4-Hr. Half-Day Trip: $300 for two people; Inshore 8-Hr. Full-Day Trip: $450 for two people. Offshore 8-Hr. Full-Day Trip: $600 for two people. All trips include beverages. Full days include lunch. All tackle provided. Board member of the Professional Fly & Light Tackle Guide's Association. Capt. Dino, 38 Berry Ave.,Staten Island, NY 10312.

Phone: 718-356-6436
fly4tuna@cs.com

WEST BRANCH ANGLER & SPORTSMANS RESORT (F)
Deposit, New York
Brown/Rainbow/Brook Trout

We offer excellent catch & release fly fishing for wild browns and rainbows. 22 upscale studio, 1-bedroom, and 2-bedroom cabins provide front door access to the West Branch, the finest tailwater trout fishery in the East. Professional Guide Service (1 guide, 2 guest ratio) is available. Fly fishing instruction also available one on one, equipment included. Accommodations are rented at a daily rate with rate determined by the size cabin.

Phone: 607-467-5525
www.westbranchangler.com

NORTH CAROLINA

FOSCOE FISHING COMPANY & OUTFITTERS (H&F)
Elk, North Carolina
Brown/Brook/Rainbow Trout/
Smallmouth Bass/Upland Birds

As an Orvis-endorsed outfitter, we offer some of the most enjoyable and scenic fishing trips to be found anywhere in the country. We gladly accept beginners to experts from ages 14 to 114. Foscoe operates our own trips year-round (weather permitting), with the best times for North Carolina being from mid-March through June and from mid-September through early November. Best times for Tennessee are from March through November, again weather permitting. We also offer upland bird hunting for grouse, turkey, and quail. 1-day, 1-person float trip, $225. 2 persons, $350.

Phone: 828-963-7431
www.foscoefishing.com

TOE RIVER LODGE (H&F)
Green Mountain, North Carolina

Brown/Rainbow/Brook Trout/
Smallmouth Bass/Quail/Pheasant/
Ruffed Grouse

A family-run business specializing in fly fishing and upland bird hunting for individuals and small groups. Fishing trips are primarily float trips for smallmouth bass and trout. Walk trips and instructional classes also available. Quail and pheasant hunting behind dogs over varied mountain terrain, or try one of our continental pheasant shoots for groups of up to ten hunters. Rustic accommodations, including a newly built timber-frame pavilion, are available. 1-day float trip: $350/2 people or $250/1 person. Half-day hunt: $200/1 or 2 hunters. Full day: $300/1 or 2 hunters.

Phone: 828-682-9335

NORTH DAKOTA

RODGERS GUIDE SERVICE (H&F)
Lake Sakakawea, Garrison, North Dakota

Walleye/Sauger/Northern Pike/Small-mouth Bass/Canada Goose/Ducks

Spring, summer and fall fishing. Lake Sakakawea is rated in the top five all-time best Walleye fisheries in North America by *In Fisherman* magazine. Daily rates: $160 per person, two person minimum. Canada Goose hunting at its finest in McLean County area in the fall. Both resident and migratory geese and ducks. Daily Rates: $150 per person per morning, 2 person minimum. Coast Guard and ND State licensed.

Phone: 701-337-5572

OKLAHOMA

SHANGRI-LA RESORT, CONFERENCE CENTER AND COUNTRY CLUB (H&F)
Afton, Oklahoma

Black Bass/White Bass/Crappie/Catfish

Shangri-La Resort and Country Club invites you to experience our fishing guide services. Grand Lake has been ranked among the top 5 lakes in the nation for largemouth and white bass fishing. Shangri-La Fishing Package includes: deluxe guest room, two boxed lunches, 4 hours fishing guide service for 2 people, boat, fuel, rod and reels, tackle, and fish cleaning.

Phone: 800-331-4060 (ext. 7319 for reservations)
www.shangrilagrandlake.com

OREGON

COLD SPRINGS OUTFITTERS (H&F)
Arlington, Oregon

Rainbow/Antelope/Elk/Mule Deer

Located in central Oregon's beautiful high desert, CSO provides fully guided hunting on 20,000 acres of private ranch property. Ranch houses with meals served family style. 5-day hunts for bull or cow elk, deer, and antelope. Bow hunt for cow elk. CSO requires a 50% deposit, with the balance due 30 days prior to arrival. If you fail to draw a tag, deposits are refundable! Hunts from $750 to $4000. Licensed, bonded and insured. Catch & release fly fishing, weekends only. Meals and lodging, only $200 per day per rod.

Rainbows up to 20 inches. Ron Cecil, Oregon Outfitters Guide #2754. PO Box 395, Arlington, OR 97812.

Phone: 541-454-2082
www.geocities.com/coldsprings-
outfitters

EAGLE CAP FISHING GUIDES (F)
Eastern Oregon and Washington
Rainbow Trout/Smallmouth Bass/ Pacific Steelhead

High-quality fishing adventure in the solitude of rural eastern Oregon and Washington. The relatively isolated and undiscovered region of these states gives anglers an opportunity for undisturbed fishing, while keeping comfortable amenities close at hand. Fishing is typically accomplished using McKenzie River-style drift boats or catarafts to float and fish the selected reach of river. Accommodations vary from riverside lodging to motels and B&Bs in rural western towns only an hour's drive from the rivers. Trip length varies from half-day to five-day outings to meet the time availability and interests of each client and prices range from $100 to $1425 per person. Example: Steelhead/float fishing for 1 person, $240. The guides are accomplished anglers in fly and spey rod fishing as well as spin and casting rod techniques. We also offer fly fishing and fly casting schools as well as instruction during the days of fishing. Trips are tailored to the needs of the anglers, from beginners to experts. Mac Huff, Orvis-endorsed guide, Frank Conley and John Sullivan.

Phone: 800-940-3688
machuff@oregontrail.net
www.wallowa.com/eaglecap

LONESOME DUCK (F)
Chiloquin, Oregon
Wild Rainbow/Wild Brown Trout

Oregon's Williamson River is noted for producing some of the largest wild trout in the country . . . and Lonesome Duck for its gorgeous guest houses on 2.5 miles of Williamson River frontage. Two log houses (sleep 6) and a restored ranch house (sleeps 4). All are fully equipped but you can still choose to have meals prepared and served in your house. Nearby are Crater Lake National Park, Lava Beds National Monument and two wildlife refuges. Come enjoy the magic of southern Oregon.

steve@lonesomeduck.com
www.lonesomeduck.com.

MORRISON'S ROGUE RIVER LODGE (F)
Merlin, Oregon
Steelhead Trout/Coho Salmon/ Chinook

Southern Oregon's premier rafting and fishing resort, Morrison's Rogue River Lodge provides a great destination for anglers, family vacations and romantic getaways. Morrison's is an Orvis-endorsed fishing lodge that has been catering to Steelhead fisherman since 1946. The best time to fish the Rogue River for the mighty Steelhead is during the fall months of September, October and November. Morrison's offers 2 to 5-day guided fishing packages, which include guided fishing, lodging and all meals. Fly fishing instruction packages available. Cottages or lodge rooms available. Dining is a consummate pleasure with gourmet cuisine at each meal. Plenty of activities for the nonangler. A fully equipped tackle, clothing and gift shop.

Phone: 800-826-1963
www.morrisonlodge.com

SUMMIT WEST OUTFITTERS (H)
Northeast Oregon
Rocky Mtn. Elk/Mule Deer

Back-country and private ranch trophy hunts. Managed, limited entry areas in the heart of some of the best Mule Deer and Elk country in the West. Comfortable camp, great food, and experienced guides. Guaranteed tag program. Rifle, bow, and muzzleloader. 5 days guided (2 on 1), $2750. Elite hunts available for 350 bulls and 200 mulies.

Phone: 541-567-6215
www.summitoutfitters.com

PENNSYLVANIA

BIG MOORE'S RUN LODGE (F)
Coudersport, Pennsylvania
Brook/Brown/Rainbow Trout/
Smallmouth Bass

Located in the north-central part of Pennsylvania, the lodge guides on 800 miles of public streams such as the headwaters of the Allegheny River, Susquehanna River and Kettle Creek. We also have our own private trophy stream with the 20 flow-stabilizing stream projects that allow us to fish year-round for stream-bred Brooks, Browns and Rainbows of all sizes: av-

erage 2–7 lbs. Also some great smallmouth bass fishing in season. Fly fishing only catch and release. Orvis endorsed.

Toll-free: 886-569-3474
Phone: 814-647-5300
Fax: 814-647-9928
bigmoores@out-doors.com
www.bigmoores.com

CAMP LITTLE J LODGE (H&F)
Pennsylvania's Allegheny Mountains
Rainbow Trout/Brown/Pheasant/
Chukar/Quail/Whitetail Deer

Dural Orvis-endorsed fly fishing and wing shooting lodge/trophy whitetail deer. Operated by Paradise Outfitters and located near State College, PA. Outstanding sporting lodge within easy driving distance of all major metro areas in the east. Deluxe accommodations, fine cuisine. Experience fabulous year-round fly fishing on totally private spring-fed creeks and rivers for trophy-size rainbow and brown trout as large as 10 lbs. with our partners Angling Fantasies. Field and continental hunts for pheasant, chukar and quail are conducted on nearly a thousand acres of prime bird habitat. 36-station sporting clays course and lighted 5-stand. Private instruction available. Trophy whitetail hunting on 1,000-acre preserve with average SCI score over 150 last three years.

Phone: 800-282-5486
www.toparadise.com

HIGHLANDS LODGE (H)
Pennsylvania's Laurel Highlands
Whitetail Deer

Operated by Paradise Outfitters and nestled in the Laurel Mountains of Somerset County, PA, the 4,000 square-foot Highlands Lodge offers all the comforts of home in a rustic, retreat setting within easy driving distance of all major metro areas in the east. Hunt trophy whitetail deer on 1,000-acre preserve with average SCI score over 150 last three years including several 200+ monsters. Hunt packages including lodging, meals and guide begin at $2,495 for management deer and $3,900 for trophy-class.

Phone: 800-282-5486
www.huntersparadise.com

PARADISE LODGE (H&F)
Pennsylvania's Allegheny Mountains
Rainbow Trout/Brown Trout/ Pheasant/Chukar/Quail/Whitetail Deer

Dual Orvis-endorsed fly fishing and wing shooting lodge/trophy whitetail deer. Operated by Paradise Outfitters and located near State College, PA. Outstanding sporting lodge within easy driving distance of all major metro areas in the east. Deluxe accommodations, fine cuisine. Experience fabulous year-round fly fishing on totally private spring-fed creeks and rivers for trophy-size rainbow and brown trout as large as 10 lbs. with our partners Angling Fantasies. Field and continental hunts for pheasant, chukar and quail are conducted on nearly a thousand acres of prime bird habitat. 36-station sporting clays course and lighted 5-stand. Private instruction available. Trophy whitetail hunting on 1,000-acre preserve with

average SCI score over 150 last three years.

Phone: 800-282-5486
www.toparadise.com

SOUTH CAROLINA

DELTA GUIDE SERVICE (F)
Georgetown, South Carolina
Red Drum/Sea Trout/Stripers/Freshwater Bass

We specialize in shallow saltwater fishing for red drum, sea trout and stripers. We also guide for largemouth bass. We have 50+ miles of totally undeveloped coastline that is made up of state or federal game preserves. We are 36 miles south of Myrtle Beach and 60 miles north of Charleston. 8-hour trip is $350 for two people. 5-hour trip is $300 for two people. Prices include all licenses, tackle, etc. Everything except your food and drinks. We can also arrange lodging, which is not included in our charge.

Phone: 843-546-3645
www.deltaguideservice.com

SPECKDRUM CHARTERS (F)
Mount Pleasant, South Carolina
Redfish/Speckled Trout/Bluefish/ Spanish Mackerel/Ladyfish/Jack Crevalle/Tarpon/Spadefish/False Albacore

Speckdrum Charters care of Bill Glenn offers fly and ultralight-tackle fishing for Redfish year-round. Speckled Trout, Jacks, Tarpon and the fall "False Albacore Blitz" off Cape Lookout, NC, are also some of the many opportunities that are available.

Speckdrum Charters is located near Charleston, SC, and can accommodate up to 3 anglers. Rates are as follows: Half Day, 4 hours, $350. 3/4 Day, 6 hours, $375. Full Day, 8 hours, $475. Wear appropriate shoes, clothing and bring your food and drink.

Phone: 843-884-8627
wbglenn@bellsouth.net

SOUTH DAKOTA

DAVE SPAID GUIDING (H&F)
Pierre, South Dakota
Pheasant/Sharptail/Prairie Chicken/ Waterfowl/Walleye/Smallmouth Bass

Fish our world-class walleye waters year round, where daily catches of 30 to 50 fish are not uncommon. Combine that with our state's finest traditional wild bird hunting in the afternoon. Seventeen years' experience. All-inclusive 3-day combination trip is $1800. Single-species packages and daily trips are also available. Call for details.

Phone: 605-224-5009
Fax: 605-945-0093
dave@davespaid.com
www.davespaid.com

FORESTER RANCHES (H)
Chamberlain, South Dakota
Upland Birds/Waterfowl

Our family-owned ranches are located in the heart of South Dakota's best pheasant and waterfowl hunting areas. We also offer prairie chicken, sharptail grouse, Hungarian partridge, dove, and turkey hunting. Our 3D/4N with hunt packages begin at $995 per person, with lodging, meals, bird cleaning. John Forester.

Phone: 605-734-5009

HORSESHOE K RANCH (H)
Kimball, South Dakota
Grouse/Pheasant

25,000-acre, private land, family-owned and -operated ranch. 3D/3N Packages available. Includes lodging, meals, bird processing, guides, dogs and license. Groups of 6–16, family or corporate. Dihl and Joanne Grohs.

Phone: 605-778-6714
hkranch-0001@easnet.net

PHEASANT CREST LODGE (H&F)
Kimball, South Dakota
Wild Pheasant/Sharptail Grouse/ Prairie Chicken/Walleye/ Smallmouth Bass

Spring Combination: fishing/wingshooting. Fall: wingshooting. Abundant wild-bird populations and vast expanses of prime habitat make for truly spectacular hunting and fishing. At the 6000-square-foot log lodge, top-rated accommodations, home-cooked food and wonderful Midwestern hospitality round out the ultimate vacation. Packages range from $750 for fishing packages to $2497 for our all-inclusive world-class pheasant hunt. 2- or 3-day vacations with lodge rooms having double occupancy. Brian Havlik.

Phone: 800-350-6340
hunting@pheasantcrest.com
www.pheasantcrest.com

STAR VALLEY LODGE & HUNT (H)
Ideal, South Dakota
Upland Pheasant/Grouse

Star Valley is a first-class lodge located in the heart of pheasant country in South Dakota. At the lodge, which accommodates up to 15 guests, you will receive deluxe treatment and great hunting. Sporting clays, experienced guides, Labrador retrievers, and warm kennels for your own dogs. After your hunt, relax in the hot tub and sauna. Deluxe 3D/4N Package is $1595 per person for 8 or more people. Season is from early Sept. to late Mar. Transportation to and from the Winner or Pierre airport.

Phone: 605-842-3853
valley@gwte.net
www.star-valley.com

TORREY LAKE HUNTING LODGE (H)
Platte, South Dakota
Pheasant

South Dakota's premiere pheasant hunts, located near Platte, South Dakota. We offer a world-class pheasant hunting experience for groups of 8–14 hunters. The ideal corporate retreat. Exclusive use of our lodge with 8 bedrooms, 8 baths, great food, equipment, guides and dogs will insure your South Dakota hunting adventure. A five-rooster minimum per day per hunter is included in our 3-day, 3-night, all-inclusive hunt package. A private, quality hunt that will meet your expectations! Our price of $2400 per hunter includes all amenities based on double occupancy. Hunt Sept. 1 through Mar. 30. Reservations are required. Please visit our website at then pick up the phone for your reservation. We look forward to discussing your hunt package.

Phone: 605-336-8301
www.torreylake.com

TUMBLEWEED LODGE (H)
Harrold, South Dakota
*Pheasant/Sharptail Grouse/
Waterfowl/Prairie Chicken/
Hungarian Partridge*

Located on 10,000 private acres in central South Dakota, Tumbleweed Lodge offers a tremendous upland bird hunting experience second to none! Host of the annual South Dakota's Governor's Hunt. Our five-star ranch-style atmosphere is well suited for the discriminating sportsman, with vast numbers of birds last seen in the 1950s. Complete accommodations include lodging, first class meals, field transportation, licensing, shells, game processing and professional guide service. 10% discount for groups 8 or more.

Phone: 800-288-5774, 605-875-3598
www.tumbleweedlodge.com

ULTIMATE OUTDOOR ADVENTURES (H)
South Central South Dakota
*Pheasant/Waterfowl/Prairie Chicken/
Sharptail*

We invite you to experience an awesome pheasant wingshooting experience. 4483 acres of habitat dedicated to and managed exclusively for hunting awaits your arrival. 20 years of outfitting experience further assures you that our staff's hospitality, accommodations, meals and overall service will exceed your expectations. If you are looking for a place to hunt in South Dakota that offers unbelievable bird counts, spectacular scenery, first-rate accommodations, more great food that you can eat, and a staff that makes your stay down right fun . . . then look no further. Book early because we have a 90% rebooking rate and dates are limited.

Phone: 888-840-7929
www.roosters4u.com

TENNESSEE

BUCHANAN RESORT (F)
Paris Landing, Tennessee
Crappie

Kentucky Lake from mid-Sept. –Oct. offers an outstanding opportunity for its famous slab-size crappie and even largemouth bass. Located on Eagle Creek, off the Tennessee and Big Sandy Rivers, this provides the best fish habitat on Kentucky Lake. Waterfront cottages. 3D/4N packages available for 2 people, including lodging, guide, bait, licenses and meals.

Phone: 901-642-2828

CEDAR ROCK HUNTING PRESERVE (H)
Shelbyville, Tennessee
Quail/Pheasant/Chukar/Turkey

When it comes to upland game birds, you can't beat the hunting at Cedar Rock. Guides, dogs and plenty of game will be furnished. Bring a friend, relative or client for a day of excitement and guaranteed shooting. For the opportunity to harvest two pheasants and eight quail: $150. For additional quail, $6.50 per bird. Pheasant: $20 per bird. We guarantee plenty of shooting. No bag limits. Morning hunts, 8:30 AM; afternoon hunts, 1:00 PM. Guided Turkey Hunts: $200 per person.

Phone: 800-680-5964
cedarrock94@aol.com
www.cedarrockhunting.com

FISHING WITH JACK WADE (F)
Knoxville, Tennessee
Striper

Top water fishing at its finest, beginning late March into May. Live bait only late May through Sept. Trophy time late July into Sept. Per day prices for 1–3 persons: $150/$300, depending on season. Lodging and meals not included. Deposit required. Call Jack.

Phone: 865-947-8018
jwadefisherman@aol.com
www.jwfish.cjb.net

GARY ROBERTS OUTDOORS FISHING GUIDE SERVICE (F)
Kingsport/Knoxville, Tennessee
Striper Hybrid

If you are looking for the fishing experience of a lifetime and you want to catch lots of big stripers and hybrid, come fish with me in the beautiful mountain lakes of Northeast Tennessee. The fish average 10 to 15 pounds with

20- and 30-pound fish common. My largest striper is 51 pounds and I am the lake record holder (Striper 47 lbs.) and the Tennessee state record holder (Hybrid 23 lbs.). The cost per day does not include lodging and meals, although available. References upon request.

Phone: 540-679-5129

groberts@naxs.net

TEXAS

BLANCO CREEK RANCH (H)
Sabinal, Texas

Superior Genetics Whitetail Deer/ Turkey/ Wild Boar/Javelina/Bobcat/ Quail/Dove

4,000 acres of Whitetail paradise located in South Texas. The 7,200-square-foot lodge and gourmet meals garnish a five-star rating. Year-round protein-managed bucks commonly score 160 and up. Other game is in abundance as well along the Sabinal River. This ranch is quickly becoming the hot new place for monster bucks in South Texas. Call for pictures. 3D/4N Package: $4500 per person and up. Observer rates $100 per day per person. Package includes guides, meals, open bar, caping animals, airport transfers. 2D/2N Package: $500 per person wild boar hunt, unlimited animals. 2D/2N Package: $600 per person Spring Turkey hunt. Susan Moulton.

Phone: 800-523-9036, 210-828-6509

COVERED GATE LODGE (H)
Southwest Texas

Whitetail/Quail/Turkey

Guided hunts. Comfortable lodging, great food. 9200 acres of excellent wildlife country. Near 100% success rate on buck deer. Typical B&C scores from 130 to 170. Also, one of the best quail preserves anywhere! Approx. 1000 acres designed and dedicated for the best quail hunting possible. Excellent dogs and guides.

Office: 210-256-0050
Ranch: 830-278-2802
Fax: 210-256-0080
coveredgateranch@yahoo.com

LAKE AMISTAD MARINA (F)
Del Rio, Texas

Largemouth Bass/Smallmouth Bass/ Stripers/Channel Catfish/Crappie

Enjoy the ultimate floating fish camp . . . a luxury houseboat rental from Forever Resorts' Lake Amistad Marina! Known as one of the best largemouth bass fisheries in Texas, at Lake Amistad you can fish from sunup to sundown without the hassle of a crowded boat ramp—just step off the back deck and into your fishing boat! Each houseboat sleeps 10 in five queen beds and is equipped with all the amenities of home, including gas grill, coffee maker, full-size range, microwave, TV, VCR, central A/C and 2 refrigerators. We even provide linens and pots and pans! It's the perfect floating fish camp! Rates start at $995 for 4 days/3 nights midweek . . . that's $95 per person for 4 days! Highway 90 West, HCR-31, Del Rio, TX 78842.

Phone: 800-255-5561
www.foreverresorts.com/HFD

LONE STAR GUIDE SERVICE (F)
Jasper, Texas

Largemouth Bass/Crappie/White Bass/ Stripers/Hybrids

With experienced and knowledgeable guides on both lakes (Toledo Bend and Sam Rayburn), Lone Star Guide Service has the ability to put you on the fish. Our guides are TP&W licensed and fish 200-plus days a year. We have packages for everyone from the beginning angler to the tournament fisherman. All trips are first class to ensure an enjoyable experience. All guide boats are equipped for safety and comfort. We can accommodate small or large groups. We have bass boats for smaller parties and a party barge that can accommodate up to eight people for larger groups. All equipment can be supplied or you are welcome to bring your own. We can even help with lodging arrangements if you like (Bass Buster Inn: 409-698-3002). Whatever your needs are, Lone Star Guide Service has you covered.

Toll free: 888-700-9889

MARINA AT LAKE MEREDITH (F)
Fritch, Texas
Largemouth Bass/Smallmouth Bass/Crappie/Walleye/Catfish

Enjoy the ultimate floating fish camp . . . a luxury houseboat rental from Forever Resorts' Marina at Lake Meredith—home to the Texas-record Smallmouth Bass and Walleye and the fly rod record for Largemouth Bass! Fish from sunup to sundown without the hassle of a crowded boat ramp—just step off the back deck and into your fishing boat! Each houseboat sleeps 10 in five queen beds and is equipped with all the amenities of home, including gas grill, coffee maker, full-size range, microwave, TV, VCR, central A/C and 2 refrigerators. We even provide linens and pots and pans! It's the perfect floating fish camp! Rates start at $995 for 4 days/3 nights midweek . . . that's $95 per person for 4 days! End of Sanford Yake Road, Fritch, TX 79036.

Phone: 800-255-5561
www.foreverresorts.com/HFD

MARK'S GUIDE SERVICE (F)
Alba, Texas
Largemouth Bass/Stripers/Hybrids/White Bass

Come fishing on Lake Fork, America's hottest bass fishing lake, with your licensed professional full-time guide, Mark Woodruff. To make your day as enjoyable as possible, Mark uses only state-of-the-art equipment. He specializes in teaching, working with beginners and children. He also specializes in the "big fish" baits and techniques, and many of his customers have caught fish weighing 10 lbs. and over. For stripers and hybrids, Mark will take you to nearby lakes Tawakoni and Cooper. Can accommodate large group trips. For lodging, he will help you obtain reservations at Fisherman's Cove. Call Mike. 579 E. Holley St., Alba, TX 75410.

Phone: 903-765-9033
woodruff@lcii.net

PEAK-A-BOO OUTFITTERS (H)
Dalhart, Texas
Mule Deer/Antelope/Waterfowl/Pheasant/Blue Quail/Turkey/Varmint

Located in the high plains of the Texas panhandle, this remote area hosts over 500,000 wintering waterfowl.

Grasslands and grain fields provide opportunities for wild pheasant, blue and bobwhite Quail. A limited number of hunts available for trophy mule deer and antelope. Deluxe accommodations, gourmet dining, skilled guide and top-notch dogs await you for the "experience" you won't soon forget. 3D/4N Combo Hunt: $1295.00.

Phone: 806-384-2210
Fax: 806-384-2215
texhunts@xit.net

RAYBURN COUNTRY RESORT (F)
Lake Sam Rayburn, Texas
Trophy Bass

Nestled in the heart of East Texas on the shores of Lake Sam Rayburn, Rayburn Country Resort is a quiet lakeside haven of unmatched beauty. We are headquarters for many of the top fishing tournaments in the country, and we also feature a 27-hole championship golf course. Special Executive 4D/3N Fishing & Golf Package: $420 (tax included) per person, double occupancy includes condo accommodations, or $340 (tax included) per person double occupancy includes hotel accommodations; 2 half-day professionally guided fishing trips; 2 half days of golf (green fees and shared cart); and pick-up and return to Jasper County Airport. Bob Almand.

resort@mail.jas.net

ROUGH CREEK LODGE EXECUTIVE RETREAT & RESORT (H&F)
Glen Rose, Texas
Upland Birds/Fishing

A world-class facility thoughtfully placed on 11,000 rolling acres in the North Texas countryside. This elegant resort offers five-star quality guest-rooms, dining and service—and features guided upland bird hunting and fishing. 60 of the finest trained dogs will assist in the hunting of quail, pheasant, chukar, Hungarian partridge or mallard duck. Once your day of hunting is complete, you may want to try your luck at fishing on the 80-acre lake using one of the four bass boats. 3D/2N 4-Hunt; Package: $1999 per hunter, Sunday–Monday. $2199 per hunter, Tuesday–Saturday. No bag limits or per-bird charges. Package includes accommodations, all meals, 4 hunts (mixed bag or quail), fishing, sporting clay or five-stand, use of fitness center and pool. Flighted mallard and European driven pheasant hunts can be added at an additional charge with 8 or more hunters.

Phone: 800-864-4705
www.roughcreek.com

RUNNING M RANCH (H)
Fowlerton, Texas
Whitetail Deer/Rio Grande Turkey/ Wild Boar/Javelina/Bobcat/Quail/ Dove

Located in the heart of huge Texas whitetail deer country, this 7000-acre ranch with 9 miles of Frio River frontage offers the best in South Texas deer hunts at an affordable price. Kept as a family secret for over 100 years this ranch has only been commercially hunted the past two years, and is producing excellent quality bucks, as well as other fine trophy animals. Still family-owned and -operated, you will experience true Texas hospitality in a cozy ranch house that comfortably sleeps up to six. 3D/4N Package: $3500 per person. Includes guides, all meals, beverages, one buck. Susan Moulton.

Phone: 800-523-9036, 210-828-6509

TEXAS SALTWATER ADVENTURES (F)
Upper/Middle Texas Coast
Deep Sea & Bay Fishing

Year round saltwater fishing at its finest. Experience a day fishing the rich Gulf waters for the many species Texas has to offer: trophy red snapper, king mackerel, dolphin fish, cobia, spotted sea trout, bull redfish and flounder. Whether you are a tournament angler or an average fisherman, we have the fishing experience for you. Full-day and half-day trips available. Please visit our web site for further information on pricing and details:

Phone: 832-428-3340 (home)
       713-605-1750 (pager)
leaf@texassaltwaterfishingguide.com
www.texassaltwaterfishingguide.com

UTAH

FALCON'S LEDGE (H&F)
Altamont, Utah
Flyfishing/Wingshooting/Falconry

The ultimate retreat for your escape and relaxation, Falcon's Ledge is located in the seclusion of the Rockies just $2\frac{1}{2}$ hours from Salt Lake City International Airport. The diversity of this country provides magnificent fishing and the setting of the lodge itself is spectacular. The Uinta Mountain Primitive Area, with peaks over 13,500 feet high, is our two-million-acre backyard, with vast tracts of untouched pine and hundreds of crystal clear lakes filled with trophy browns, rainbows, brooks and cutthroats. We also offer upland bird hunting for chukar partridge, Chinese ringneck pheasants, ruffed grouse, sage grouse and doves. In the afternoons, enjoy a falconry safari for a once-in-a-lifetime memory as we put a falcon on your fist. Corporate groups welcome.

Toll free: 877-879-3737
falcon@ubtanet.com
www.falconsledge.com

TRIPLE H HUNTING (H&F)
Salem, Utah
Elk/Deer/Moose/Sheep/Antelope/ Lion/Pheasant/Trout

Trophy hunts on private and public draw areas. Comfortable accommodations, good food, experienced guides. 5-day 1x1 guided hunts. We have over 50,000 acres of private land in Utah and Nevada. Guaranteed permits on most hunts, in Utah and Nevada limited draw areas. 90% success on all hunts. Elk: $4800; Moose: $3800; Deer: $3800; Antelope: $1750; Lion: $3500; Fishing: $200/day. Bruce.

Phone: 801-423-1142
Fax: 801-423-3259

UNITED STATES OUTFITTERS UTAH (H)
Utah
Elk/Mule Deer/Sheep/Moose/ Mountain Lion

USO has built a tremendous reputation in the hunting industry by hunting the best areas of the Rockies. By guaranteed private land tags as well as draw tags, USO's clients harvest more trophy-class animals than any other outfitter in the nation each year. Archery, muzzleloader, and rifle hunts available. USO handles all the applications through their "professional licensing service" and fronts much of the license cost to their hunters in order to apply to multiple quality areas to have the best chance of obtaining a real trophy hunt. Very comfortable accommodations, great food. Normally no horseback required. Hunt costs are $3450.

Phone: 800-845-9929

www.huntuso.com

WADE LEMON HUNTING (H)
Holden, Utah
Mule Deer/Elk/Bear/Mountain Lion/ Bison/Antelope/Bobcat

At Wade Lemon Hunting, we are committed to quality trophy hunts. Our staff consists of some of the most committed and dedicated sportsmen you will ever meet. They are the best in their field. We have the Use Permits required by the U.S. Forest Service and Bureau of Land Management to guide and operate legally throughout most of the state of Utah. We operate on 3 ranches that equal over 150,000 acres of private land under Utah's Cooperative Wildlife Management Unit Program. This allows us longer, more liberal seasons and guarantees mule deer and elk tags on some trophy areas. We also have exclusive cougar and bear hunting rights on several hundred thousand acres. My family has been ranching

and hunting a lot of this country for the past 15 years. There is much beauty and history in this land. Come let me share with you what I call "God's Country."

Phone: 435-795-2299

VERMONT

FOUR SEASON ANGLERS GUIDE SERVICE (F)
Pawlet, Vermont
Trout/Salmon/Lake Trout/Bass/ Northern Pike/Woodcock/Ruffed Grouse

Vermont is blessed with a wide variety of fishing opportunities for cold- and warm-water species. Pristine rivers for trout and lakes for salmon, lakers, bass and pike. Fly fishing or spinning, all abilities. *Beginners are welcome!* Learn to fly fish with patient on-stream instruction. Also, fall woodcock and grouse hunts over a pointing dog followed by winter ice fishing adventures. Vermont is a spouse-safe destination. Daily trips are 4 to 8 hours, with hot meals on full days. Rates include equipment, tackle, flies or lures. Call Orvis-endorsed guide Chuck Kashner.

Phone: 800-682-0103

WISCONSIN

BOULDER LODGE OUTFITTERS (H&F)
Hayward, Wisconsin
Muskie/Whitetail Deer/Bear/ Waterfowl/Grouse

Come fish northern Wisconsin's Ridgeland, which separates water flowing south to the Mississippi River and north to Lake Superior. The geological uniqueness of this area in the Cheqamagon National Forest provides many different lakes, rivers, and streams that offer a variety of fishing opportunities, from steelhead and trout to muskie, walleye, and bass. With such an abundance of different waters and fisheries, our guide Dan Edwards can instruct the beginner or challenge the expert, in a comparable setting. This area is described by the U.S. Forest Service as "steeped on cultural heritage . . . displaying unique cultural diversity and traditions dating back as early as 1000 B.C." Come on up and experience our fishing, hospitality and beautiful country. Visit the Fly Box with fishing equipment and apparel along with outdoor merchandise. Don't forget to bring your camera!

Phone: 888-462-3002
www.boulder-lodge.com

ROSS' TEAL LAKE LODGE & TEAL WING GOLF CLUB (H&F)
Hayward, Wisconsin
Muskie/Walleye/Northern Pike/ Crappie/Smallmouth Bass/ Largemouth Bass/Grouse

In northwestern Wisconsin, on timeless Teal Lake, is a fishing lodge reminiscent of bygone era, yet right up to the minute (AAA 3 diamond). While muskie fishing is as good as ever on the Quiet Lakes (Teal and Lost Land, the only two lakes in the Midwest with a 10-mph speed limit and *no* skiing) Ross' Teal Lake now also has an adjacent championship-level golf course, Teal Wing GC. You can fish, golf, eat and sleep at a superior quality of each, without ever getting in the car! What more can a sportsman ask for?

Phone: 715-462-3631
rossteal@cheqnet.net
www.teallake.com

WHITETAIL WONDERLAND (H)
Wisconsin
Trophy Whitetail Deer

WW is divided by open meadows, stands of hardwoods and deep coulees—a fantastic location, adorned with breathtaking fall colors, and the residents are Trophy Bucks which rival any in the world. Superior genetics, strict game management and ample food allow these deer to grow enormous racks. The hunts range from $1500–$8000 (125–200 Class). Axis Adventures.

Phone: 800-363-4909
www.trophydeer.net

WYOMING

ANTELOPE OUTFITTERS (F)
Buffalo, Wyoming
Mule Deer/Antelope/Elk/Whitetail Deer

Small, highly successful, long-time Wyoming outfitters. 100% success every year on antelope, 85% on mule deer, and 85% on 6 x 6 bull elk. Team Realtree Pro Hunter. Private ground hunts. See hundreds of animals daily. Archery, rifle, handgun or primitive. We don't sell hundreds of hunts each year, only a few select hunts with great results.

Phone: 307-684-5609
www.antelopeoutfitters.com

BOULDER LAKE LODGE (H&F)
Pinedale, Wyoming
Trout/Elk/Mule Deer/Antelope/Moose

Nestled in the heart of the Bridger-Teton National Forest, Boulder Lake Lodge offers a secluded location for family vacations, corporate retreats, lodging and meals. The accommodations are rustic, yet fully modernized, with a maximum capacity of 34. Meals are served "ranch style," with all you can eat! Horse pack trips are available for fishing, big game hunting and horse trekking. Trips range from just a few days in our 10,000-foot fishing camp to a 10-day excursion through the Wind River Mountains. We feature friendly, highly experienced professional guides and excellent mountain-savvy livestock. Free brochure available.

Phone: 800-788-5401
blodge@coffey.com
www.boulderlake.com

BRIDGER WILDERNESS OUTFITTERS (H&F)
Pinedale, Wyoming
Elk/Moose/Bear/Antelope/Trout/ Arctic Grayling

Over 17 years' experience offering top-quality guide service for hunting and fishing. Hunting: Excellent success on all hunts. Specializing in classic Western-style horseback hunts from remote camps or from our lodge. Fishing: Top-quality wilderness fishing pack trips for 6 types of trout and arctic grayling. Drift fishing on the Green and New Fork rivers. Pack Trips: Both fishing and sightseeing pack trips offered. Guest Ranch Packages available through our Historic DC Bar Guest Ranch.

Phone: 307-367-2268
www.bwo.com

BRUSH CREEK RANCH (H&F)
Saratoga, Wyoming
Trout/Trophy Mule Deer/Trophy Elk

Brush Creek Ranch is a 6000-acre working cattle and guest ranch nestled at the foot of southern Wyoming's spectacular Snowy Range Mountains. Outstanding fly fishing with over 3 private miles of Brush Creek awaits you, as well as float and wade fishing on 140 miles of the blue-ribbon freestone waters of the upper North Platte and Encampment rivers. Private trophy ponds, an abundance of high mountain lakes and streams as well as two tailwater sections of the Platte at the Miracle Mile and Grey Reef make unsurpassed variety. 4N/3D Fishing Package: $1250 per person, double occupancy. Our private trophy hunts offer a legitimate chance at a 180-point-plus trophy mule deer as well as trophy-class elk. Guided Mule Deer Hunt: 5D/6N Package, $2500. Guided Elk Hunt: 5D/6N Package, $3000.

Phone: 800-726-2499

DARBY MOUNTAIN OUTFITTING (H&F)
Big Piney, Wyoming
Mule Deer/Elk/Moose/Bighorn Sheep/ Antelope/Black Bear/Mountain Lion/ Cutthroat/Brook/Rainbow

Come to beautiful Wyoming and enjoy quality, first-class, full-service hunting, fishing and horseback pack trips at an affordable price. At Darby Mountain Outfitting we are dedicated professionals who put forth the extra effort (experience blended with personal service) to assure you will enjoy your stay with us. We want it to be an experience worth returning to. For free brochures, information, and prices, write to: Box 447, Big Piney, WY 83113.

Phone: 307-386-9220

DC BAR GUEST RANCH (F)
Pinedale, Wyoming
Trout/Arctic Grayling

Located adjacent to the Bridger-Teton National Forest where three mountain ranges come together. In the upper valley of the Green River, the ranch sits at 8000 feet in elevation in alpine meadows where the aspen and pine trees come together. Spectacular views of the Wind River Mountains, Wyoming's tallest and wildest. Individual cabins scattered in a timbered setting. Beaver pond and wildlife. Excellent fishing.

Phone: 307-367-2268

www.bwo.com

DOUBLE DIAMOND OUTFITTERS (H)
Salt and Grey River Drainages, Wyoming

Mule Deer/Elk/Moose

Hunt these steep, rugged, trophy-producing areas from our high-county pack-in tent camp located at approximately 8500 feet in elevation. Our success is attributed to our knowledgeable guides, hard work, and abundant resident herds. Big game, dedicated guides, scenic hunting grounds, dutch-oven cooking, and gentle horses guarantee a memorable and exceptional hunting experience. 6-day guided (2 on 1) mule deer hunt, $2895. Reed "Rick" Miller. Lic. #010, hunting Bridger-Teton National Forest.

Phone: 307-885-4868

www.doublediamondoutfitters.com

DOUBLE DIAMOND OUTFITTERS #010 (H)
BLM, Bridger-Teton and Caribou National Forests, Wyoming

Mule Deer/Elk/Antelope/Moose/ Mountain Lion

Hunt western Wyoming's abundant big game from our modern yet rustic log ranch-style accommodations. Archery or rifle. We travel to nearby trailheads, hunt resident herds and re-turn to your warm comfortable accommodations in the evening. We offer dedicated, hard-working knowledgeable guides, scenic hunting grounds, western hospitality, dutch-oven cooking and memorable hunting experiences. All affordably priced with 3-day antelope or cow elk starting from $995 and 5-day ranch accommodations bull elk or mule deer hunts from $2595.

Phone: 307-885-4868

www.doublediamondoutfitters.com

FRED MAU'S OUTDOOR ADVENTURES (H&F)
Cheyenne, Wyoming, and Worldwide

Big Game/Fishing/Waterfowl/Upland Birds

Fred Mau's Outdoor Adventures offers hunting and fishing adventures worldwide specializing in Russia, Canada, Mexico, Australia, Africa, Mongolia, Argentina and of course, the United States, including Alaska. Species include elk, whitetail, mule deer, antelope, bear, moose, sheep, mountain lion, turkey, waterfowl, upland game, and big game fish, just to mention a few. We personally inspect every outfitter that we represent and take pride in our high customer satisfaction.

Phone: 800-470-5511

Fax: 307-778-7173

fmoa@fmoa.com

www.fmoa.com

GREAT ROCKY MOUNTAIN OUTFITTERS (F)
Saratoga, Wyoming

Wild Brown Trout/Rainbow/Brook/ Cutthroat

Orvis-endorsed. Located in un-crowded south-central Wyoming since 1981, Great Rocky Mountain Outfitters offers float and wade trips for trophy wild brown, rainbow, brook and cut-throat trout on over 140 miles of the blue-ribbon freestone waters of the spectacular Upper North Platte and En-campment rivers. Dry and wet fly fish-ing available April through October. In addition, the Miracle Mile and Gray Reef areas of the Platte offer year-round trophy tailwater fishing. Private river and trophy pond leases, as well as a multitude of mountain streams and lakes, round out a diverse fishing expe-rience for the beginner and expert alike. The complete Orvis shop will supply all your tackle needs and will personalize a package trip to your special require-ments. Day trips and overnight expedi-tions available. Personable guides. 20 years of professional service. Corporate groups welcome. Inquire for prices on daily trips or overnight fishing pack-ages in our sportsmen's cottages.

Phone: 800-326-5390
www.grmo.com
www.rivercottages.com

LEE LIVINGSTON OUTFITTING (H&F)
Cody, Wyoming
Elk/Mule Deer/Bighorn Sheep/ Moose/Trout/Grizzly Bear Viewing/Wildlife Photography

Three wilderness hunting camps, two bordering Yellowstone National Park on the east and 50 miles from Cody. The third camp is in the Elk Fork Drainage, which is 40 miles from Cody. Lee Livingston is the only outfitter per-mitted to hunt these drainages. Each has over 100 square miles of territory. The lodge hunts are conducted from a ranch west of Cody near Yellowstone Park. You may hunt right from the ranch or trailer horses to a nearby trailhead. Ma-jor factors in our hunting success are our locations, accommodations, food, guide, horses and an abundance of wildlife. Hunting prices range from $1500 to $6000. We also offer pack-trips, just $200 a day per person. Tro-phy fishing trips are $250 a day per per-son, which includes a specialized trout fishing guide. Trips usually run 4 to 8 days, depending upon the individuals.

leliving@wyoming.com

Q CREEK LODGE (H)
Mills, Wyoming
Mule Deer

A magnificent, comfortable guest ranch nestled in the Shirley Mountains of Wyoming. A wealth of wildlife, in-cluding one of North America's pre-mier trophies: heavily antlered mule deer. 3D/4N Packages available with guides. Contact Steve Steinle.

Phone: 307-356-4200

RIMROCK RANCH (H&F)
Cody, Wyoming
Elk/Mule Deer/Bighorn Sheep/Moose/ Cutthroat/Rainbow/Brook/Brown/Lake Trout

Two wilderness camps, both offering superb elk, deer, bighorn sheep and moose hunting opportunities. In the last 9 years, we've had 433 gun elk hunters kill 350 bulls; 95% of those killed were 5x5's or better. Archery elk hunts run $3500. Rifle elk hunts run $3800 to

$5000. Gary Fales has been in the outfitting industry since 1963 and provides experienced guides and mountain horses for his hunters. We also have pack trips/fishing trips for $200/day per person. The pack trip season runs from June to the first part of September with progressive trips ranging from 4 to 8 days. Call Gary and Dede Fales.

Phone: 800-208-7468
rimrock@wyoming.com
www.rimrockranch.com

RON DUBE'S WILDERNESS ADVENTURES (H&F)
Northwest Wyoming
Elk/Moose/Bighorn Sheep/Mule Deer/ Cutthroat

Old-fashioned horseback pack train adventures 24 miles from road's end into the famous Thorofare Region. Our comfortable tent camp, with separate cook, dining, sleeping and dedicated shower tent, is located only $1\frac{1}{2}$ miles from the east boundary of Yellowstone Park. Unsurpassed fishing for native cutthroat trout averaging 17–18 inches. World-class wilderness big mulie bucks. Fish in July and August. Rifle elk Sept.–Oct. Also late season 3-day bull or cow elk hunts, from lodge, from $1000 per person, November and December. Lic. #BG033.

Phone: 307-527-7815
Fax: 307-527-6084
joshua@huntinfo.com
www.huntinfo.com/dube

THUNDER MOUNTAIN OUTFITTERS (H&F)
Jackson Hole/Wind River, Wyoming
Shoshone and Bridger-Teton Forests
Elk/Bear/Deer/Lion/Antelope/Moose/ Trout

Spring and fall big game hunting. Fair chase. Two permitted camps in pristine elk habitat. Summer and fall fishing in lakes, streams and rivers. Also fishing out of lodge and back-country camps. Member, Wyoming Outfitter Assn., Member, Dubois Outfitters Assn., Jackson Hole Outfitters Assn. Call for further information.

Phone: 307-455-2225
Fax: 307-455-2031
info@trianglec.com

TRIANGLE C RANCH (H&F)
Jackson Hole/Wind River, Wyoming
Elk/Bear/Mt. Lion/Moose/Deer/Trout/ Antelope/Sheep

Fall hunting. Shoshone and Bridger-Teton Forest permits. All big game 7-day trophy hunts from $4000 per person, one on one. Lake and River Trout fishing, $250 per day in camp with guide on horseback. Deluxe camp accommodations, excellent food. Archery and rifle. We are a fair chase outfit. We promise 100% effort to insure the best opportunity for a successful and enjoyable hunt. Low hunter numbers in camp! Thunder Mountain Outfitters, Rocky Mountains, Wyoming.

Phone: 800-661-4928
Fax: 307-455-2031

TWO OCEAN PASS OUTFITTING (H&F)
Moran, Wyoming
Cutthroat/Brook/Rainbow Trout/ Elk/Mule Deer/Antelope/Black Bear/ Mountain Lion/Bighorn Sheep/Rocky Mtn. Goat

Hunt on horseback the famous Two Ocean Pass Country, Teddy Roosevelt's favorite big game hunting area. Experience the best cutthroat trout fishing anywhere and our summer pack trips into Yellowstone National Park and the Teton and Washakie Wilderness Areas. All of which are designed and planned for the satisfaction of each group. Fishing video available: "ESPN Fly-fishing the World." Guiding and outfitting have been a way of life for the Winter family since 1946. We are committed to quality service and success. John R. Winter, Outfitter.

Phone: 307-543-2309
dwinter@wyoming.com
www.wyoming.com/~topwyo

UNITED STATES OUTFITTERS WYOMING (H)
Wyoming
Elk/Sheep/Moose/Mountain Goat

USO has built a tremendous reputation in the hunting industry by hunting the best areas of the Rockies. By guaranteed private land tags as well as draw tags, USO's clients harvest more trophy-class animals than any other outfitter in the nation each year. Archery, muzzleloader, and rifle hunts available. USO handles all the applications through their "professional licensing service" and fronts much of the license cost to their hunters in order to apply to multiple quality areas to have the best chance of obtaining a real trophy hunt. Very comfortable accommodations, great food. Hunt costs are $3450.

Phone: 800-845-9929
www.huntuso.com

YELLOWSTONE OUTFITTERS & WAGONS WEST (H&F)
Afton and Jackson Hole, Wyoming
Trophy Cutthroat Trout/Trophy Elk

Deluxe Trout Fishing: 6-day horse pack trips on the headwaters of the Yellowstone and Thorofare Rivers in the Teton Wilderness next to Yellowstone Park. Trophy wild breed cutthroat trout, in the 16–20 inch (3–4 pound) class. Catch and release. We are an Orvis-endorsed Expedition Outfitter, and this is truly a fly fisherman's paradise. Experience the thrill of packing in with horses and mules. 6-day or longer scheduled trips offered. Deluxe tent camps with excellent full-course meals. Cooks, packers and guides included. Everything furnished except your fishing gear, sleeping bag and personal gear. $1375 per person. Trophy elk hunts on the Yellowstone Meadows, next to the southeast corner of Yellowstone Park. Bugle season rifle hunts, 10-day rifle hunts, $4400. 7-day rifle hunts, $3600. Also we operate Wagons West Covered Wagon Treks all summer. All trips originate from our base camp on the Buffalo River at Turpin Meadows, 45 miles north of Jackson Hole next to the Teton Wilderness Area.

Phone: 800-447-4711
www.recworld.com/yellowstone

CANADA

ALBERTA

ALBERTA TROPHY DEER (H&F)
Central Alberta, Canada
Trophy Whitetail/Mule Deer/Brown Trout/Rainbow Trout

Hunt Alberta's trophy whitetail and mule deer! November rut hunts from heated, elevated, fully enclosed stands and ground blinds. Territory in central Alberta includes private and public land. Combination and single-species hunts available. Now booking for next year. Guided, full-service 6-day hunts starting at $3250 US. Add fall fishing on your choice of 3 blue-ribbon trout streams early in the hunting season. brown trout and rainbows to remember for a lifetime.

Phone: 866-258-2945
adventures@albertawild.com
www.albertawild.com

ALBERTA WILD ADVENTURES (H&F)
Canadian Rockies, Alberta, Canada
Upland & Migratory Birds/Elk/Mule Deer/Whitetail Deer/Black Bear/ Cougar/Varmint/Trout/Northern Pike/Whitefish/Walleye

Sporting adventures on the eastern slopes of the Canadian Rocky Mountains to the northern boreal forests in Alberta. Hunt our pristine wilderness on foot, ATV, or horseback, spot and stalk on thousands of square miles of farm land. Fishing opportunities too numerous to list, three blue-ribbon trout streams. Sample 4N/3D Package: 1 day fishing by canoe in the rapids and pools of Red Deer River, 1

day wading and walking mountain streams, 1 day hunting upland game birds or varmints in the foothills— $1150 per person, dbl occp. Includes accommodations, meals, guides and transportation. Licenses extra. His & Hers or Father/Son packages.

Phone: 866-258-2945
adventures@albertawild.com
www.albertawild.com

ANDREW LAKE LODGE AND CAMPS (H&F)
Northern Alberta, Canada
Black Bear/Trophy Canadian Moose/ Northern Pike/Lake Trout/Walleye

Discover trophy hunting in the northernmost part of Alberta on the border of the Northwest Territories. We exclusively hunt this remote wilderness area of over 5000 square miles. Hunt for some of Alberta's largest Black Bear and Canadian Moose. Trips can be combined with trophy fishing for Northern Pike, Lake Trout and Walleye. Television features by major networks. Alberta's finest fly-in trophy fishing and hunting. Fully guided 7-day hunts: Moose, $4250 US; Bear, $2950 US.

Phone: 866-258-2945
adventures@albertawild.com
www.albertawild.com

AWESOME ACCESS (F)
Canadian Rockies, Alberta, Canada
Brown/Rainbow/Brook/Bull/Lake Trout/Northern Pike/Rocky Mountain Whitefish/Walleye

Fishing adventures on the rivers, lakes and streams of the Canadian Rocky Mountains in Alberta. Awesome

Access provides the excitement of fishing by canoe in the white water of the Red Deer River, driftboats on the blue-ribbon Bow River, fly fishing the blue-ribbon Crowsnest River, and much more. We accommodate fishermen/women of all levels of experience and ability. Sample 7N/6D Package: 2 days by canoe, 2 days by driftboat, and 2 days in high mountain lakes and streams—$2450 per person, dbl occp. Includes accommodation, meals, guides and transportation & license. His and Hers or Father/Son packages, and lessons.

Phone: 866-258-2945
adventures@albertawild.com
www.albertawild.com

COUGAR OUTFITTERS (H)
Alberta, Canada
Cougar/Mule Deer/Whitetail Deer

Cougar is one of North America's finest trophies. Each hunter has two guides that have been in the cougar-hunting business for 20 years, 15 of their cats have made B&C, and they have guided over 120 successful hunts. Hunts are based out of a ranch-type setting. 4x4, quads and snowmobiles are used for these hunts. Experience a quality hunt in the splendor of Western Alberta's foothills and the Canadian Rocky Mountains.

Phone: 866-258-2945
adventures@albertawild.com
www.albertawild.com

FISH TALES FLY SHOP (F)
Southern Alberta, Canada
Rainbow/Brown/Cutthroat/Bull Trout

Whether you're planning a quick stop on a business trip or in search of a multiday, hardcore angling trip, Fish Tales can supply your southern Alberta adventure. Join our seasoned guides for a day on the world-famous Bow River casting to Browns and Rainbow Trout. Walk and wade for Cutthroat in nearby mountain streams, or venture to the Elk River area of southwestern BC for a chance to land big Bulls and Cutthroat trout. You tell us what you want and we'll do our very best to accommodate your needs. Prices start at $450 per day/2 fishers.

Phone: 866-258-2945
adventures@albertawild.com
www.albertawild.com

FLY-IN ICE FISHING ADVENTURES (F)
Northern Alberta, Canada
Northern Pike/Lake Trout/Walleye

Fly in for a unique ice-fishing adventure on remote lakes in northern Alberta. Fish for trophy-class Northern Pike, Lake Trout, Walleye, Perch and Whitefish. Light housekeeping and full-service packages include air charter, accommodations, and snowmobiles. Season: March 1 to April 15. 3D/4N Package includes air charter from Ft. Smith, N.W.T., starting at $700 US. Northern hospitality and an abundance of wildlife will make a trip with us one you will remember forever.

Phone: 866-258-2945
adventures@albertawild.com
www.albertawild.com

LELAND LAKE CABINS & OUTPOST CAMPS (F)
Northern Alberta, Canada
Northern Pike/Lake Trout/Walleye

Incredible fly-in sports fishing in northern Alberta's shield country. Exclusive camps on pristine lakes where Great Northern Pike, Lake Trout and Walleye dominate. Catching trophy fish exceeding 20 lbs. is not uncommon. Spring, summer and fall seasons with self-catering and full-service packages. Sample package: 3 days including air charter from Ft. Smith, N.W.T., $575 US. Hundreds of square miles per fisherman—a sporting adventure you will never forget.

Phone: 866-258-2945
adventures@albertawild.com
www.albertawild.com

OVERALL OUTFITTING (H)
Alberta, Canada
Bighorn Sheep/Elk/Whitetail/Mule Deer

We offer you 21 years of experience in the guiding and outfitting industry. Our rifle and archery elk camps are in comfortable tents with wood stoves, during the rut. Bighorn sheep season is Sept. 1–Oct. 15 in the Red Deer and Bighorn drainages of the Canadian Rocky Mountains. We offer deer hunts in Nov. when the monarchs are in full rut. Accommodation for deer hunts is a log cabin with wood stove on our own farm. All hunts can be a two-animal combination. Wolf, coyote and varmint hunts can also be arranged.

Phone: 866-258-2945
adventures@albertawild.com
www.albertawild.com

WAYBACK OUTDOOR ADVENTURES (H&F)
Eastern Slopes of Canadian Rockies, Alberta, Canada
Shiras Moose/Elk/Whitetail Deer/ Mule Deer/Rainbow/Cutthroat/Bull Trout/Upland and Migratory Birds

Fantastic trout fishing on the eastern slopes of the Canadian Rocky Mountains. Fair chase elk, deer, upland and migratory bird hunts in fall, varmint (prairie dogs) in spring and summer. Cast and blast available. Wilderness camps, riverside lodges, cabins and B&B available. Member of APOS, Rocky Mountain Elk Foundation, Safari Club International. Lots of activities for the whole family, historic tours, hiking, horseback riding. Let us design your custom adventure.

Phone: 866-258-2945
adventures@albertawild.com
www.albertawild.com

WESTERN ADVENTURES (F)
Canadian Rocky Mountains, Alberta, Canada
Rainbow/Cutthroat/Bull Trout

Fish mountain streams and lakes in the beautiful Canadian Rocky Mountains by horseback. Stay in our comfortable outfitters tents complete with carpet, beds and wood heaters. Experience western hospitality around the campfire, enjoy hearty meals cooked on a wood stove and served in our spacious cook tent. Send some of the family horseback riding for the day or everyone ride to Window Mountain Lake and spend the afternoon casting into clear mountain waters. Close to many activities, we specialize in family packages.

Phone: 866-258-2945
adventures@albertawild.com
www.albertawild.com

BRITISH COLUMBIA

AVNORTH AVIATION 2000 (H&F)
Nimpo Lake, British Columbia
Wild Rainbow/Lake Trout/Bull Trout

An air charter service consisting of two DCH-2 Beavers, one C-185, and one C-180, all on floats. We have a five unit inn plus luxury cabins all situated on the waterfront of beautiful Nimpo Lake. Guests have a choice of either fishing for wild rainbow trout, from 1–7 lbs. right on Nimbo Lake, or enjoy a flight out to one of our many fly-in-only lakes and rivers. For those wilderness adventurers who want to take care of themselves, we will fly you into a remote outpost log cabin, setup for housekeeping located on a great fishing lake. All fishing is non-guided. We also offer scenic flights over spectacular glaciers, breathtaking Hunlen Falls, and tours of the mountain ranges with an opportunity to see abundant wildlife. Hunting packages can also be arranged.

Phone: 250-742-3285, 250-742-3303
Fax: 250-742-3238

THE BLACKWATER COMPANY (F)
Interior British Columbia, Canada
Rainbow Trout

Six-day wilderness float trips through the boreal forest of the Fraser River Plateau in central British Columbia. Two separate trips on the upper or lower Blackwater River assure fantastic dry fly fishing throughout the mid-June to late September season. One guide and boat for each two anglers, and a camp crew that proceeds ahead of the group to prepare all camp comforts (including endless hot shower).

Common catch rates of 50 rainbow trout averaging 14 inches await fly fishers, and generous time is spent wading. Upper river, early season trips $2995 (incl. fly-in), lower river $2695.

Phone: 541-318-8769
www.theblackwater.com

CHILCOTIN HOLIDAYS LICENSED ANGLING GUIDE & GUEST RANCH (F)
Gold Bridge, British Columbia
Rainbow Trout/Dolly Varden/Brook

Whether you're a trout fishing enthusiast with a custom rod or a beginning angler with an urge to hook a magnificent rainbow trout, Spruce Lake will fulfill your dream. Spruce Lake teems with a natural population of native rainbow trout. With its extensive shoreline shallows, Spruce Lake is ideal for fly fishing and spin casting. You'll strike many fish, and your guide will cook them to order. As well as tips on the best flies to use, your licensed angling guide is knowledgeable on wildlife and the environment. Accommodation is our high alpine camp, located on the shore of Spruce Lake. We have spacious tent cabins, and our pioneer log cabin provides a fully serviced cookhouse. Fishing licenses available on site.

Phone/Fax: 250-238-2274
adventures@chilcotinholidays.com
www.chilcotinholidays.com

HAGGARD COVE RESORT (F)
Barkley Sound, Vancouver, British Columbia
Salmon/Halibut/Bottom Fish

17 years in operation. Secluded shoreline accommodations for up to 10 guests. Directly in the path of huge

schools of migrating Salmon. Dozens of "calm water" (no swells) fishing hotspots are within 10 minutes of the lodge. The fishing is done on 24- to 28-foot boats with local, experienced guides. Delicious home-cooked meals are served family style 4 times a day with fresh seafood the specialty. All-inclusive 4-day/3-night packages June through September, from $850 per person. Call for reservations or a free video.

Phone: 250-723-8457

KYLLO BROS. OUTFITTING 1954 (H&F)
Hudson's Hope, British Columbia
Moose/Mountain Goat/Caribou/
Black Bear/Grizzly Bear/Dolly
Varden/Rainbow/Bull Trout

Summer fishing for Dolly Varden and bull trout to 20 lbs. and rainbow trout to 5 lbs. 5-day packages from $1350 per person. Spring Black Bear and grizzly hunting and fall hunting. Our exclusive 2400-square-mile hunting area is located in the Musqaw Range of the Rocky Mountains. Hunt for moose, mountain goats, caribou, black bear, and grizzly bear. 10-day packages from $4900 per person. Charter member of the Northern B.C. Guides Association.

Phone: 250-783-5248
Fax: 250-783-5510
kyllo@pris.bc.ca
www.kylloadventures.bc.ca

MOOSE LAKE LODGE (H&F)
Chilcotin Coast, British Columbia
Moose/Black Bear/Grizzly Bear/Wolf/
Steelhead/King Salmon/Coho Salmon/
Pink Salmon/Sockeye Salmon/
Chum Salmon/Rainbow/Cutthroat/
Dolly Varden/Halibut

Orvis-endorsed fly fishing lodge, featuring daily floatplane fly-outs, guided fly fishing on the famous Dean River for steelhead and salmon, and dry fly fishing on the Blackwater River. Fish a different river each day from floatplane or helicopter. 3- to 7-day packages from $1350 to $4000 per person. Hunt moose, black bear and wolf. 10-day packages from $4990 per person. John Blackwell.

Phone: 250-742-3535
Fax: 250-742-3749
www.mooselakelodge.ca

NORWEST GUIDE OUTFITTERS (H)
Cranbrook, British Columbia
Elk/Mountain Goat/Grizzly Bear/
Black Bear/Mule Deer

NorWest Guide Outfitters offers one-on-one guide service within Purcell Wilderness Conservancy located in Southeastern BC. Base camps are log cabins, with some tent camps. Base camp is 2 hours' back-roads drive from Cranbrook. Horse and hiking. 2 to 3 hunters per camp, total 12–18 hunters per year in area. Member, Rocky Mountain Elk Foundation and Guide Outfitters of British Columbia.

Phone: 250-426-5230
threebarsranch@cyberlink.bc.ca

ONE EYE OUTFIT (H&F)
Chilcotin Region, British Columbia
Grizzly Bear/Black Bear/Mountain
Goat/Moose/Mule Deer/Rainbow Trout

One Eye Outfit has provided quality hunting and fishing expeditions for 20 years in the Chilcotin Region of British Columbia. We hunt grizzly bear, black bear, mountain goat, moose and mule deer with excellent success records and hunter references. We fish for native rainbow trout in a world-class designated fishery. We also provide alpine tours and wilderness outpost camp holidays in southeast boundary of spectacular Tweedsmuir Provincial Park. We use floatplanes, boats and horses to get around and we give our clients an authentic, hospitable Western experience in the mountains.

Toll free: 866-398-8329
oneeye@wlake.com

RENDEZVOUS ISLAND LODGE HELICOPTER FISHING (F)
British Columbia, Canada
Rainbow, Cutthroat and Steelhead Trout and Dolly Varden

At Rendezvous Island Lodge in British Columbia, you will enjoy outstanding mixed-bag fishing via helicopter for rainbow, cutthroat, sea-run Dolly Varden and steelhead, surrounded by white peaks and evergreen valleys—the essence of British Columbia's wilderness. In the midst of all this rugged and striking country you will also enjoy *not* "roughing it." Rendezvous Island Lodge provides intimate five-star comfort, gracious personal service and outstanding food and beverage for exclusive parties of 8 anglers. 5N/4D fishing package: $3495 per angler, double occupancy. Air travel, liquor and tips not included.

Phone: 800-211-4753
www.rodgunresources.com

THREE BARS CATTLE & GUEST RANCH (F)
Cranbrook, British Columbia
Trout

Three Bars Ranch offers upscale guest ranch facilities and activities to our 40 guests per week. Our location in the Canadian Rockies is perfect for all our activities, including horseback riding, guided hikes, tennis, indoor pool, hot tub, campfires, volleyball and raft trips. St. Mary's River is just a 20-minute hike from lodge. Local fly fishing guides pick you up at the lodge for river float fishing or wade trips.

Phone: 250-426-5230
threebarsranch@cyberlink.bc.ca
www.threebarsranch.com

MANITOBA

ACE WILDERNESS GUIDING (H&F)
Thompson & Gillam, Manitoba, Canada
Black Bear/Moose/Whitetail/Walleye/ Northern Pike

Trophy Manitoba Black Bear spring or fall hunts, 100% opportunity since 1992, 25% record book bear, 25% color phase bear. Archery or gun. Area extends over 2400 square miles with 40 active bait sites. Camp consists of 4–6 hunters and 2–4 guides. 6-day all-inclusive package: $2200. Fly-in Moose. Fall combo hunts—moose, bear, wolf, fishing. "Our area records speak out." 1997 Manitoba #1 P&Y scored $188\frac{3}{8}$! 1998 Manitoba B&C scored $210\frac{5}{8}$! Our success rate remains at 75%++. 6-day all-inclusive package: $6000. Archery Whitetail. Interlake area of Manitoba holds more Pope & Young records than any other province. 6-day all inclusive package: $1600. Fishing Manitoba's north is noted for exceptional fishing for northern pike and walleye. Fishing is available at no extra charge during hunts. Virgin waters 88 air miles from nearest town. August fly-in fishing packages, 6 days all inclusive: $1000. Art and Ellen Henry.

Phone: 204-383-5628
hunting@mb.sympatico.ca
www.manitobahunts.com

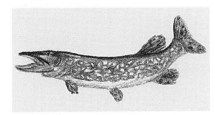

BIG SAND LAKE LODGE (F)
Manitoba, Canada
Northern Pike/Lake Trout/Arctic Grayling/Walleye/Moose/Black Bear

Big Sand Lake is over 70 miles long and our lodge is the only one on the lake, providing you with over 60,000 acres of pristine waters to fish. American Plan packages include round-trip air from Winnipeg to the lodge. Licensed and experienced guides, new 18-foot boats with 40-hp/4-stroke outboard motors. Accommodations in fully modern spacious log cabins, gourmet food and daily shore lunch. Choose among 4, 7 and 8-day packages. We also operate 4 mini-lodges where we have combined the comforts of a main lodge with the freedom of an outpost camp. The locations are for groups of 6–10 people. A full-time camp manager and cook are on hand to free up valuable fishing time. Call today for details. We'd love to send you one of our free CD-Roms, videos or brochures.

Phone: 800-348-5824
www.bigsandlakelodge.com

DESJARDINS OUTFITTING SERVICE (H)
Laurier, Manitoba, Canada
Trophy Bear/Whitetail Deer

Hunt Manitoba's Black Bear along Riding Mountain National Park. $1600 US for a 6-day hunt, spring or fall. Licenses, lodging, meals and travel to and from baits included. Contact Alexis Desjardins. Box 9, Laurier, Manitoba, Canada ROJ 1A0.

Phone: 204-447-3028

HEALEY'S GODS LAKE NARROWS LODGE (F)
Gods Lake Narrows, Manitoba, Canada
Northern Pike/Whitefish/Walleye/ Brookies/Lake Trout/Sturgeon

Healey's Gods Lake Narrows Lodge is on famous Gods Lake, where the fishing is world class and the wilderness is yours. Arrive in Winnipeg at your convenience. We provide deluxe cabins, fine food and a "homey" atmosphere. Unsurpassed are our scenery, fishing and wildlife. Healey's Gods Lake Narrows Lodge is a family-run business. We make it a point to get to know all our guests and to provide any service which will make your trip more enjoyable. As a family, we have been in the area for more than 20 years.

Phone: 800-353-9993
www.godslake.com

KASKATTAMA SAFARI ADVENTURES (H&F)
Hudson Bay, Manitoba, Canada
Waterfowl/Brook Trout

A truly world-class lodge "Where the Flyway Begins." Deluxe accommodations for only 16 guests at a time. Our September hunts showcase 8 species of geese, 12 species of ducks and upland game hunting for ptarmigan. All-inclusive, full-service American Plan package: 5 days for US $2295 including charter flights from Winnipeg. Photo opportunities for caribou, moose, black bear and polar bear. Taiga helicopters based at lodge throughout the season. Contact Charlie Taylor.

Phone: 204-667-1611
kaska@sympatico.ca

LAURIE RIVER LODGE & KAMUCHAWIE OUTPOST (H&F)
Lynn Lake, Manitoba, Canada
Trophy Northern Pike/Walleye/Lake Trout/Bear

Guests at Laurie River Lodge have exclusive rights to the Laurie River System (a tributary to the mighty Churchill) and several of the lakes in the area southwest of the town of Lynn Lake. Our American Plan lodge on McGavock Lake can accommodate 32 fishermen in private, fully modern, solid log cabins. Our guests enjoy professionally prepared gourmet dinners, hearty breakfasts, daily shore lunches, complimentary hard liquor bar, professional guides and free after-dinner fishing. We offer fishermen the choice of 4- and 8-day trips on private charter flights from the town of Saskatoon, Saskatchewan. For fishermen who like it a little rougher we have a do-it-yourself outpost on Kamuchawie Lake. Spring black bear hunts also available.

Phone: 800-426-2533

MOLSON LAKE LODGE (H&F)
Northern Manitoba, Canada
Trophy Northern Pike/Walleye/ Lake Trout/Bear/Moose

With three species of trophy-size fish—northern pike, walleye and lake trout—complemented by unsurpassed service, it is no wonder that guests of Molson Lake Lodge are 90% repeat or referral. Enjoy the convenience of being able to leave almost anywhere in the US and be fishing in northern Manitoba that same afternoon. Our chartered 45-passenger aircraft departs Winnipeg and flies direct to our 4500 foot airstrip. Molson Lake is 30 miles long and 12 miles wide and we are the only lodge on the lake. Fishing season, mid-May through mid-September; hunting in spring and fall. American Plan and outpost camp rates available. Video upon request. Lyle and Dianne Fett, PO Box 493, West Fargo, ND 58078.

Phone: 800-521-1347
Fax: 701-282-6093
starsafaris@compuserve.com
www.molson-lake.com
www.safaris-inc.com

NUELTIN FLY-IN LODGES (F)
Manitoba/Northwest Territories, Canada
Trophy Lake Trout/Northern Pike/ Arctic Grayling

Nueltin was the first lake in Canada to institute a catch-and-release policy in 1978. More than 27 rivers and streams feed the 120 miles of this remarkable body of water. Exclusive access to 40 anglers a week. Fly-in only! 300 miles from the nearest road! New equipment every year.

Modern comfortable private cabins. Easy access aboard our comfortable chartered direct flight from Winnipeg, Manitoba (included in all packages). The most professional management, guides and support staff in the industry. Family-owned and -operated with more than 20 years' experience in the hospitality industry. 7D/7N Package: $3295 per person. Shawn Gurke.

Phone: 800-361-7177
www.nueltin.com

TRAPPER DON'S LODGE AND OUTFITTING SERVICES (H)
Manitoba, Canada
Trophy Black Bear/Trophy Whitetail/ Canadian Moose

Enjoy Manitoba's wilderness! 25 years of operation with experienced licensed guides. Full professional service from your home and back. We are a very small, personalized outfitter taking a maximum of 6 hunters per week at our camps. Because of our size, we are able to customize our hunting trips to meet the expectations of our clients. Don McCrea.

Phone: 204-569-4833
www.cyber-resort.com/trapperdon/

TUCK'S HUNTING (H)
Manitoba, Canada
Whitetail Deer/Waterfowl/Upland Birds

Tuck's Hunting is your key to the most spectacular waterfowl, upland game bird and whitetail deer hunting in North America. Located on the west side of Manitoba along the Saskatchewan border in the Duck Mountains. Some of the largest whitetails in the province come from this area every year (in excess of 200 inches B&C). We hunt from gentle horses, treestands and 4x4 trucks. Our bird hunting is equally good, with large flights of Canada and snow geese as well as ducks. We also offer upland bird hunting for sharptail and rough grouse. Prices: 6D/7N whitetail hunts, $2500 US per person plus license and tax. Birds, $400 US per day per person plus license and tax. (Minimum 3 days/4 nights.)

Phone: 204-256-8992
Fax: 204-255-5101
tuck@autobahnaccess.com

WHITESHELL OUTFITTERS (H&F)
Rennie, Manitoba, Canada
Trophy Whitetail/Black Bear/Deer/ Ducks/Geese/Ruffed Grouse/Spruce Grouse/Walleye/Northern Pike/Yellow Perch

We're famous for our trophy whitetail deer. Come hunt the ridges and forests of the beautiful Whiteshell area. Offering exclusive, full-service whitetail hunts limited to 4 persons per week and a maximum of 12 in a year. We specialize in bow hunting and also welcome both rifle and muzzle hunters. Our remote-access outcamps are warm and comfortable. We're a small, family-run business that truly customizes hunts to our guests. With over 20 years of guiding experience, we'll make your wilderness hunt in Manitoba a memorable one. A 6-day all-inclusive package for archery and muzzle loader is $1800. Rifle, $2000. We also now offer black bear/fishing combos: 6 days, $1600.00. We meet our guests in Winnipeg and from then on their only concern is the hunt or the fishing. We look after everything else.

Toll free: 877-302-5322
Fax: 204-369-5651
whiteshelloutfit@aol.com

WILDERNESS BEAR GUIDES (H)
Thompson, Manitoba, Canada
Trophy Black Bear/Whitetail

Trophy Manitoba Black Bear spring or fall hunts, 100% opportunity since 1992, 25% record book bear, 25% color phase bear. Archery or gun. Area extends over 2400 square miles with 40 active bait sites. Camp consists of 4–6 hunters and 2–4 guides. Drive up on paved road, or commercial jets arrive daily at Thompson and Gillam. 6-day all-inclusive package: $2200. Manitoba's north is noted for exceptional fishing for Northern Pike and Walleye. Fishing is available at no extra charge during hunts. Art and Ellen Henry.

Phone: 204-383-5628
hunting@mb.sympatico.ca
www.manitobahunts.com

NEWFOUNDLAND

MINIPI RIVER SYSTEM (F)
Labrador, Canada
Brook Trout

The last place on earth where large numbers of 5 to 8-pound brookies can be taken on dry fly! This is the same fishery explored by Lee Wulff and

Curt Gowdy in the 1950s & 1960s and reported on the "American Sportsman." Unlike other once-great trophy brook trout locations, the Minipi River has been protected and preserved throughout the years. Access for a limited number of fly fishermen each year is all that's available. Seven nights, six days of fishing—$3295. Call for more information.

Phone: 888-347-4896

OWL'S NEST LODGE (H)
St. John's, Newfoundland, Canada
Moose/Woodland Caribou/Black Bear
Special new rates. Group discounts available. Special early fall bow season. Rifle, bow and black powder. Exclusive accommodations for Bowhunters. 95%–100% success rate for moose and caribou. All-terrain vehicles (4- and 8-wheelers) and boats provided. We own and operate 14 different lodges (plus spike camps). Spring black bear up to 600 lbs. Woodland caribou not subject to migration. Contact Ronald Parsons.

Phone: (W) 709-722-5100
      (F) 709-722-0808
      (H) 709-368-9013
info@owlsnestlodge.com
www.webpage.ca/owlsnest

NORTHWEST TERRITORIES

KASBA LAKE LODGE (F)
Northwest Territories, Canada
Lake Trout/Northern Pike/Arctic Grayling
Kasba Lake is located 800 miles north of Winnipeg, Manitoba, a $2\frac{1}{2}$ -

hour flight on a 50-passenger aircraft. Spectacular Northern Pike to 30 lbs., huge lake trout to 50 lbs., feisty arctic Grayling to 5 lbs. Accommodations are above average: two bathrooms per cabin, carpet on floors, propane heat. Great meals, shore lunches, guides, new 40-hp, 4-stroke motors. Boats with casting decks and swivel seats. We are catch and release Fly fishing comes naturally at Kasba in addition to spinning gear. Packages are all-inclusive except personal purchases, airfare to Winnipeg and gratuities.

Toll free: 800-663-8641
kasba@kasba.com
www.kasba.com

PLUMMER'S ARCTIC LODGES (F)
Canadian Arctic
Trophy Lake Trout/Arctic Char/Arctic Grayling
Plummer's Arctic Lodges operates one lodge on Great Slave Lake, all the lodges on Great Bear Lake, and camps on the Tree and Coppermine Rivers. These waters hold the IGFA all tackle world records for lake trout (72 pounds), arctic char (32 pounds) and arctic grayling (5.9 pounds). Not only will you enjoy some of the world's finest trophy fishing but you will also receive some of the best service as well. Packages are all-inclusive from Winnipeg or Edmonton with direct Jet Service right to the lodges in the heart of Canada's Arctic. It is an experience few are lucky enough to enjoy.

Phone: 800-665-0240
www.plummerslodges.com

ONTARIO

BEAR'S DEN LODGE (H&F)
French River Delta, Ontario, Canada
Black Bear/Freshwater Fish

Remote and secluded—boat or float-plane access only. Combo black bear Hunting and Fishing Package available, including a 7-day guided hunt; 7 nights accommodations in modern facilities a boat, motor, gas and oil for fishing over trophy waters; excellent home-cooked meals; and skinning and freezing of your trophy. Fishing packages available for trophy muskie, northern pike, walleye, bass, crappies, catfish and pan fish. Full American Plan packages available. Our 7-night/7-day fishing packages include double occupancy, home cooked meals, boat, motor, gas and oil, and daily maid services. Taxes, licenses, and gratuities are extra. Your hosts are Art and Brenda Barefoot.

Phone/Fax: 705-857-2757
Winter phone/fax: 814-839-2443
bearsden@bedford.net
www.bearsdenlodge.com

CROW ROCK LODGE (F)
Lake of the Woods Kenora, Ontario, Canada
Northern Pike/Walleye/Lake Trout/ Smallmouth Bass/Largemouth Bass/ Muskie

A first class boat-in lode 17 miles south of Kenora. World-class fishing for bass, walleye, muskie, pike, and trout amongst 14,500 islands and unlimited shoreline. Fish 8 remote lakes and be the only angler on the lake! Comfortable 17' bass style boats with quiet Honda motors. Clean and comfortable waterfront cabins with superb dining. 3-Day packages available. Al Lindner from *In-Fisherman* magazine says: "Crow Rock Lodge is centrally located on Lake of the Woods for some of the finest muskie, smallmouth and walleye fishing in the world. Unique to Crow Rock are private little lakes on the island that hold smallmouths when the weather's too rough on the Woods. The guides here are good, knowledgeable anglersm the lodging is superior, and the fishing can't get much better."

Phone: 800-547-FISH
www.crowrock.com

HAWK LAKE LODGE (H&F)
Northwest Ontario, Canada
Smallmouth Bass/Northern Pike

Access to Canada's finest Smallmouth Bass angling from Ontario's premier American Plan fishing lodge. The rugged, brightwater lakes of the Canadian Shield coupled with the best Smallmouth Bass angling in Northwest Ontario provide the backdrop for this spectacular, one-of-a-kind fishing lodge. One lodge, 20 lakes and limitless opportunities for the avid angler. Offering 24 guests a truly unique combination of superb, five-star accommodation, fine dining and unmatched amenities. Operating from mid-May through September. Inclusive packages US $315 pp/night.

Phone: 800-528-9045
www.hawk-lake.com

LA BELLES BIRCH POINT CAMP (H&F)
Devlin, Ontario, Canada
Bass/Pike/Crappie/Walleye/Grouse/ Duck/Bear/Trophy Whitetail

Located on beautiful Rainy Lake in Northwestern Ontario. Rainy Lake is noted for its great Smallmouth Bass and Northern Pike fishing. *In Fishermen* magazine rates Rainy Lake as the number-one Bass fishery in North America. We have excellent fall/winter Crappie fishing with some weighing over $2\frac{1}{2}$ lbs. You catch a lot of trophy Walleye and Northern up to 20 lbs. Weekly cabin rentals: 2 people, US $360; 4 people, US $975. We have a small grocery and bait store. Experienced, reliable guides. We will pick clients up at the International Falls airport for those who wish to fly. Fall Bass and Crappie fishing are excellent. Fall hunting for grouse, duck, bear and trophy whitetail deer.

Phone: 807-486-3345
labelles@fort-frances.lakeheadu.ca
www.duenorth.net/labelles

MANOTAK LODGE (F)
Northwestern Ontario

Walleye/Northern Pike/Smallmouth Bass/Muskie/Whitefish/Perch

Enjoy Northwestern Ontario's wilderness. Fantastic fishing for Walleye, Northern Pike, Smallmouth Bass, Muskie, Whitefish and Perch. We are a deluxe drive-in fishing lodge offering full American Plan or housekeeping packages that include a lakefront cabins and quality 16-foot boats with 20-hp, electric-start motors. 7-day packages from $385 per person. Chosen by *Sports Afield* as one of the greatest lodges in North America. Perrault Falls, Ontario, Canada P0V 2K0.

Phone: 807-529-3231
Toll free: 800-541-3431

manotak@moosenet.net
www.manotak.com

NEW MOON LODGE (F)
Lake of the Woods, Morson, Ontario, Canada

Walleye/Bass/Muskie/Northern Pike

Family-owned and -operated since 1957, with three generations to serve you. Known for our warm hospitality, excellent service and delicious home cooking and baking. Situated on a $4\frac{1}{2}$ acre island 12 miles by boat from Morson, Ontario. Our 4-day American Plan Fishing Package includes 4 nights lodging, daily maid service, three meals a day, and 3 days of fishing with boat, motor and guide based on 2 people in each boat, and up to 5 gal. of gas each day. Approximate cost: $675 US per person. Does not include taxes or license. Call Kathy.

Phone: 807-488-5611 (Nov.–April)
807-488-5813 (May–Oct.)

SLIPPERY WINDS WILDERNESS RESORT (F)
Yoke Lake, Northwestern Ontario

Lake Trout/Largemouth Bass/Muskie/ Northern Pike/Smallmouth Bass/ Walleye

With access to six separate lakes, Slippery Winds Wilderness Resort offers its guests the thrill of catch-and-release angling for six species in a pristine wilderness setting! Our American Plan, fly-in lodge is located only 35 air miles north of Fort Frances, Ontario. Excellent fishing, comfortable and fully modern accommodations, a friendly and professional staff and delicious home-cooked meals make the

Slippery Winds experience special. Operating from mid-May to the end of September, we accommodate a maximum of 16 anglers per trip. American Plan packages start at $850 US per person for 3 days of fishing.

Phone: 800-736-8936
www.fishcanadian.com

QUEBEC

DIANA LAKE LODGE (H&F)
Nunavik Region, Quebec, Canada
Atlantic Salmon/Arctic Char/Brook Trout/Lake Trout/Caribou/Black Bear/Ducks/Geese/Ptarmigan

Diana Lake Lodge is located 40 miles northwest of Kuujjuaq, Quebec, on a lake and river system 65 miles long that makes its way to Ungava Bay, where endless sea-run arctic char lay in icy, clear water. Besides trophy fishing for arctic char, brook trout and huge lake trout, Diana Lake Lodge also offers world-class and record-book caribou and bear and the best ptarmigan hunting in the Arctic. The lodge sits high on a treeless knoll with majestic views offers a quaint dining room, spacious living room and a French chef who will delight you with his meals! Heated platform tent cabins are warm and comfortable. We also have hot showers and flush toilets. Join our flying fisherman, hunter and bush pilot, Joe Stefanski, and Inuit hunter Isaac Angnatuk for the trip of a lifetime!

Phone: 800-662-6404
Fax: 603-532-6404
www.higharcticadv.com

HIGH ARCTIC ADVENTURES (H&F)
Nunavik, Quebec, Canada
Caribou/Upland Game/Brook Trout/Lake Trout/Arctic Char/Salmon

An outstanding adventure in Nunavik, the Canadian wilderness of northern Quebec. Combine your trophy caribou hunt with excellent ptarmigan hunting and trophy brook trout, arctic char, salmon and lake trout fishing. Our full-service, fly-in lodge and our outpost camps provide magnificent views and abundant wildlife that includes musk ox and wolves. We also offer six-day float trips down our exclusive 65-mile river for fishing, camping and photography adventures. Whatever your trip includes, do not forget your camera for wonderful photo opportunities. Bush pilot and outdoorsman Joe Stefanski continues to provide excellent results with his trophy Caribou hunts and quality fishing adventures. Our 6-night package starts at $3995 per person from Montreal. Joe Stefanski.

Phone: 800-662-6404
Fax: 603-532-6404
www.higharcticadv.com

LAKE TERNAY LODGE (H&F)
Northern Quebec, Canada
Brook Trout/Lake Trout/Northern Pike/Salmon/Black Bear/Caribou

This remote lodge, 100 miles northwest of Labrador City, Labrador, is located on a beautiful island which can only be reached by floatplane. Here we offer outstanding fishing for ouananiche (landlocked salmon), brook trout, lake trout and pike. Fishing pressure is nonexistent when you fish for these native species. You will be amazed by the numerous lakes, rivers and streams found in this most remote area of Northern Quebec. For more information, contact Joe Stefanski.

Phone: 800-662-6404
Fax: 603-532-6404
www.higharcticadv.com

LA RESERVE BEAUCHENE (H&F)
Temiscaming, Quebec, Canada
Brook Trout/Smallmouth Bass/Splake/ Walleye/Northern Pike/Lake Trout

Serious fishing in the high hills of Quebec, hard by the Ottawa River and a $4\frac{1}{2}$ -hour drive from Toronto, La Reserve Beauchene protects the splendid fishing provided by more than 30 drive-to lakes and 50,000 acres of magnificent, exclusive territory. First-rate sport with superior facilities, wonderful food and excellent service. Our guests are serious about fishing and serious about us. Moose and black bear hunting also available. Jean-Guy Dube.

Phone: 819-627-3865
www.beauchene.com

LES ENTREPRISES DU LAC PERDU (F)
Quebec, Canada
Pike/Brook Trout/Lake Trout

Come live with us the dream of a lifetime! The Lost Lake is a sportfishing heaven, teeming with fish, including lake trout, and offering a wide variety of excellent trophy species, whatever your fishing technique. In fact, it is recognized as one of the best locations in Canada to land trophies. There is also an abundance of northern pike and native brook trout. All 8 cabins of Les Entreprises du Lac Perdu look out onto the lake and can accommodate up to 8 guests comfortably. Each cabin comes with two bedrooms, an indoor toilet, a fully equipped kitchen, running water, central shower, electricity, wood- or oil-burning heating, propane stove and refrigerator. Les Entreprises du Lac Perdu is a family business that is proud to provide its guests with personalized service. Our 5D/5N nights Package is $775 US. Includes meals, lodging, boat, outboard motor, gas and floatplane transportation.

Toll free: 888-433-3505
Fax: 418-825-2113
mauclair@lacperdu.com
www.lacperdu.com

NORPAQ ADVENTURES (H)
Northern Quebec, Canada
Caribou Hunts

Based in Schefferville, the #1 destination for caribou in Ungava, Norpaq offers 3 different systems perfectly adapted to the migration patterns and to the needs of the hunters. Fully Guided (System 3) US $3599: 1 guide and 2 hunters. Includes food and cook. Semi-guided (System 2), US $2895: 1 guide and 6 or 12 hunters. Includes food and cook. Unguided (System 1) US $2495: 1 guide and 6 or 12 hunters. Food not included. Prices include 6 nights at camp and airfare from Montreal. Not included: Taxes (7.5%) and licenses.

Phone: 800-473-4650
Fax: 418-877-4652

O'SULLIVAN LAKE LODGE (H&F)
Quebec, Canada
Walleye/Northern Pike/Lake Trout/ Bear/Moose

O'Sullivan Lake Lodge rests on an exclusive, well-maintained and protected territory in the northern Outaouais region of western Quebec. The large main lake and 10 smaller lakes offer a multitude of fishing and hunting opportunities for all. Our catch-and-Release programs insure exciting and enjoyable walleye, lake trout and northern pike fishing. 7-day fishing packages start at $360 per person. Large game hunters can also experience thrilling black bear and moose hunting adventures. 7-day hunting packages start at $500 per person. Guests return year after year for trophy fish, the scenic wilderness and, our accommodations, home-cooked meals and friendly staff.

Phone: 819-441-FISH
Fax: 819-449-7394
gagnon@travel-net.com
www.travel-net.com/~gagnon

SAFARI NORDIK (H&F)
Kuujjuaq, Quebec, Canada
Caribou/Black Bear/Ducks/Geese/ Speckled Trout/Lake Trout/Northern Pike/Walleye/Atlantic Salmon/Arctic Char

Safari Nordik hunts trophy caribou among the Leaf River herd, which has had very little hunting pressure. This herd has produced a great number of record-book animals scoring 400 or more points. Our high success rate is mainly due to the fact that all our camps are situated in prime caribou country, 35 miles apart. With over 30 camps, of which we only use 9 or 10 at a given time, we have greater mobility and choice camps to send hunters to. All hunting packages are worry-free and contain no extra costs. From the moment you arrive in Montreal, we handle everything.

Phone: 800-361-3748
Info@safarinordik.com
www.safarinordik.com

SASKATCHEWAN

GLEN HILL'S SASKATCHEWAN TROPHY HUNTING & FISHING LODGE (H&F)
Tobin Lake, Saskatchewan, Canada
Walleye/Northern Pike/ Trophy Black Bear/Trophy Whitetail Deer

Located in the heart of world-class trophy whitetail deer, black bear hunting, lunker northern pike and record-class Walleye fishing in Saskatchewan, Canada. Deluxe first class lakeside 5600-sq.-ft., 12-Bedroom, 16-bathroom lodge with dish TV, pool table, fireplace and excellent home cooked meals, located in a remote area on Tobin Lake. Interested in trophies? Whether it is trophy-antlered Whitetail Deer, Lunker (large) Northern Pike, Black Bear with lots of color, or record-class Walleye over 10 lbs., trophies are what we do best. "Where the Big Ones keep getting Bigger." 5-day fishing and hunting trips available. Package prices do not include hunting licenses, fishing licenses, allocation tags, airline tickets, meals at hotel, hotel to airport pick-up, tips for cook and guide, etc.

Phone/Fax: 306-374-3223
trophies@sk.sympatico.ca
www.sasktrophies.com

HATCHET LAKE LODGE (F)
Northern Saskatchewan, Canada
Northern Pike/Lake Trout/Arctic Grayling/Walleye

If you're dreaming of a fishing adventure in which you'll catch monster northern pike or huge lake trout, Hatchet Lake Lodge will bring you one step closer to making your dream a reality! Located in the heart of Canada's most productive fishing waters, it's a fact that most guests will catch the largest fish of their lifetime during their 5-day stay at Hatchet Lake Lodge! Complete 5- and 9-day packages start at $2495 departing from Winnipeg, Manitoba.

Phone: 800-661-9183
www.hatchetlake.com

MINOR BAY LODGE & OUTPOSTS (F)
Wollaston Lake, Saskatchewan, Canada
Trophy Northerns/Lake Trout/Walleye/Arctic Grayling

Minor Bay Lodge is a remote fly-in American Plan lodge located on Wollaston Lake in northern Saskatchewan. Experienced guides ensure guests the opportunity to catch and release trophy northern pike, lake trout, walleye, and arctic grayling. To a maximum of only 26 guests, accommodations are private, fully modern cabins. Exceptional cuisine is prepared by our professional chef and served by friendly staff in our lodge dining room. The log-construction main lodge offers a guest lounge and screened veranda overlooking the lake. Daily flyouts are available to lakes reserved exclusively for our guests, use.

Phone: 888-244-7453
www.minorbay.sk.ca

SCOTT LAKE LODGE & OUTPOSTS (F)
60th Parallel—Saskatchewan/ Northwest Territories, Canada
Trophy Northern Pike/Trophy Lake Trout/Arctic Grayling

Experience the relaxed luxury of Canada's most elegant fly-in lodge. Our commitment to customer service is as extraordinary as our fishery. We take pride in our first-class approach to the entire operation: classy guest cabins, great food including complimentary house wine with dinner, experienced guides, complimentary use of quality Orvis rods and reels, comfortable $18\frac{1}{2}$-foot boats with ultra quiet four-stroke Honda outboards, daily maid service, airport and hotel pick-ups, and a private charter service from Saskatoon. Main Lodge: 4-day trip, US $2795; 5-day trip, US $3095. Packages begin in Saskatoon and include everything but alcohol, optional daily flyouts, tax and gratuities. Outpost packages also available: 4-day, US $1695; 5-day, US $1995.

Phone: 888-830-9525
Fax: 406-556-5834
info@scottlakelodge.com
www.scottlakelodge.com

WILD THING OUTFITTER (H&F)
Carrot River, Saskatchewan, Canada
Trophy Whitetail/Black Bear/Ducks/ Geese/Grouse/Partridge/Trophy Walleye/Northern Pike

We put the fun back into hunting. We're located in the northeast corner of the province and will introduce you to some of the finest trophy whitetail deer hunting in all of Canada. We also offer black bear hunts, ruffed grouse, sharptail grouse, spruce grouse, Hungarian partridge, ducks and geese. You can fish for trophy walleye and northern pike. Tim Fehr, your guide and the owner of Wild Thing Outfitter, holds the Saskatchewan record with an 18-lb. walleye caught on 6-lb. test. Tim has 22 years' experience and is a member of the Saskatchewan Outfitters Association. Sample package prices: 6-day trophy whitetail hunt, US $2800 per person 6-day black bear hunt, US $1800 per person. Both include lodging, meals, guide (2x1). License not included.

Phone: 306-768-3829

WOLLASTON LAKE LODGE (F)
Wollaston Lake, Saskatchewan, Canada
Trophy Northern Pike/Lake Trout/ Walleye/Arctic Grayling

Wollaston Lake is among the most remote fishing lakes anywhere. Angling success is assured through the lodge's long-term commitment to catch-and-release fishing. Fly nonstop on a chartered executive-class aircraft from Winnipeg directly to the lodge's airport. A team of experienced, professional guides will soon have you in the middle of some of the hottest fishing available. Five-star meals, modern cabins and a lodge with breathtaking views await you. Maximum number of guests per trip: 50. 5D/5N Packages and 9D/9N Packages with 8 full days of fishing are available.

Phone: 800-328-0628

YUKON

BONNET PLUME OUTFITTERS (H)
Trophy Dall Ram

Located in Canada's Yukon Territory, we offer exclusive guiding rights in the 7200-square-mile area accessible only by air. Once in sheep country, the hunter and his guide will do the majority of their hunting by backpack. The Bonnet Plume area has a tremendous population of Dall Sheep offering the hunter an excellent opportunity to harvest a trophy Dall Ram. 10-Day Hunt Package: $10,700 US. Includes the harvest fee for the sheep. Additional expenses: licenses, air charters, Yukon territorial trophy fees, hotel and meals before and after the hunt. We also offer Alaska/Yukon moose, barren ground caribou, wolf, wolverine, grizzly and black bear hunts.

Phone/Fax: 867-633-3366
bplume@internorth.com
www.yukonhunting.com

MIDNIGHT SUN OUTFITTING (H&F)
Yukon Plateau, Yukon, Canada
Dall Sheep/Fannin Sheep/Grizzly/ Alaska Yukon Moose/Barren Ground

and Mountain Caribou/Wolverine/
Wolf/Arctic Grayling/Arctic Char/
Northern Pike/Dolly Varden

Truly one of the most remote areas in North America—350 airmiles north of Whitehorse. The area is 12,000 square miles encompassing the Wind and the Hart River watersheds. This is the second largest area in the Yukon. Horseback and float trips are available for all game animals. Our area is fly in only with our own charter air service. We offer 23 years experience and are members of the Yukon Outfitters Assoc. Contact Alan & Mary Ellen Young, Box 4583, Whitehorse, YUKON Y1A 2R8.

Phone: 867-333-1885, 403-242-9209
Fax: 403-242-0525
msunout@telusplanet.net
www.midnightsunoutfitting.com

CARIBBEAN

BAHAMAS

ANDROS ISLAND BONEFISH CLUB (F)
Cargill Creek, Andros Island, Bahamas
Bonefish

Built on the site of a 250-year-old English sasil plantation, Andros Island Bonefish Club takes you away from it all and places you within a fly cast of some of the best bonefishing in the world. Accommodations are spacious, comfortable, air-conditioned rooms with 2 double beds and private bath. The team at the Bonefish Club is first rate. Capt. Rupert Leadon, owner/operator, has passed his enthusiasm and commitment to service onto his staff. He personally leads and trains his competent native guides, who are highly skilled and experienced saltwater flats fishing guides. We serve Bahamian dishes cooked by the best chef on the island. 7 N/6D fishing package: $2415 per week per person. Come fish with us!

Phone: 242-368-5167
Fax: 242-368-5235

BORN FREE CHARTER SERVICE (F)
Nassau, Bahamas
Deep Sea Fishing

Life is good at Born Free Charters. An adventure with us gives you the absolute best value. Whether you're an expert or novice, you'll have your best day of deep sea fishing ever as you hook into a tuna, wahoo, dolphin, or billfish. You will be fishing in 8000 to 10,000 feet of water within 20 minutes of leaving the dock. Or you may choose to go light-tackle fishing over the reefs for smaller fish, snappers, barracuda, etc. Half-day charters start at $400 (35-ft. Allman) or $600 (48-ft. Chris Craft); $800 to $1200 for a full-day charter. Prices include bait, tackle and ice; food and drinks extra. Give us a call to plan a fantastic day.

Phone: 242-393-4144
Fax: 242-394-1956
bornfree@batelnet.bs
www.born-free.com

FISH ROWE CHARTER SERVICE
Georgetown, Exuma, Bahamas
Saltwater Sportfish

Ever fished San Salvador, Rum Cay, Cat Island, Long Island, Ragged

Island or Exuma Cays? Now you can, aboard Fish Rowe (37-ft. Hatteras Sportfish). We are the only charter boat serving the southern Bahamian islands year round. So come join us for true out-island adventure and awesome marlin, dolphin, wahoo, tuna and yellow eye snapper fishing. Half days start at $550. Full days are $800. (Overnights and package deals available.) Charter includes up to 6 people, bait, ice, soft drinks, top-of-the-line tackle, captain and crew. (Gratuities not included.) Taxidermy service also provided for fish mounts. "Watch out, cause you might get hooked on Fish Rowe Charters!"

Phone: 242-345-0074
www.worldwidefishingguide.com

KAMALAME CAY (F)
Andros Island, Bahamas
Bonefish

Experience world-class accommodations and exceptional service while fishing pristine Bahamas bonefish waters on remote north and northwest Andros Island flats and the seldom-fished Joulter Cays. All-inclusive, luxurious packages reflecting value and absolute quality.

www.frontierstrvl.com

MANGROVE CAY CLUB (F)
Andros Island, Bahamas
Bonefish

Situated just steps from the Middle Bight and a short skiff ride from the west side, the Mangrove Cay Club has proven itself to be a premier bonefish lodge. Experienced management, splendid accommodations and food, solid guides and bonefish averaging 4 pounds with daily shots at fish in the 7- to 10-pound range. It's a destination not to be missed.

Phone: 800-245-1950
www.frontierstrvl.com

U.S. VIRGIN ISLANDS

MARLIN PRINCE SPORTFISHING (F)
St. Thomas, U.S. Virgin Islands
Blue Marlin

Bluewater fishing at its finest—traditional or on fly. Blue and White Marlin, Wahoo, Mahi Mahi, Tuna and Sailfish. Marlin season is June through October. June 1st–Nov. 1st (7:30am–5:30pm), $1200. Year-round (8:00am–4:00pm), $1000. Half-day inshore fishing for Kingfish, Bonito, Barracuda (4 hrs.), $550. Trips for up to 6 people. Gratuities not included.

Phone: 340-693-5929
Fax: 340-774-8958
marlinprince@viaccess.net
www.marlinprince.com

TOM McQUADE GUIDE SERVICE (F)
St. John, U.S. Virgin Islands
Bonefish/Tarpon/Permit

Saltwater fly fishing. Bring your tennis shoes: wade fishing only—the way fly fishing was meant to be. Fish for Bonefish, Tarpon and Permit. 20 years' experience. Half day (6 hours) $300. Includes gear, guide and flies. Lodging is available. Tom McQuade, PO Box 161, St. John, USVI 00831.

Phone: 340-693-9446, 340-693-8300

SOUTH AMERICA AND CENTRAL AMERICA

ARGENTINA

ESTANCIA BELLA VISTA (F)
Rio Gallegos River, Argentina
Sea-Run Brown Trout

Fishing for sea-run brown trout and resident brown trout on miles of the Rio Gallegos and on several tributaries. The average sea-run fish is 6–8 pounds, but trout of 20–25 pounds are taken each season on the Gallegos.

Phone: 800-245-1950
www.frontierstrvl.com

FLORO LAVALLE OUTDOORS (H&F)
Argentina
Rainbow Trout/Brown Trout/Lake Trout/Dorado/Red Stag/Axis/Fallow Deer/Black Buck/Asian Buffalo/Puma/European Wild Goat/Ducks/Geese/Doves/Pigeons/Partridge

Experience *the* finest dove, waterfowl, big game hunting and fishing in the world with Floro Lavalle, a fifth-generation Argentine who will share Argentina's culture on some of the family-owned estancias, of which one has its own private 18-hole golf course. Dove shooting with no limit, no season. Duck, goose and partridge from April to August. More than 15 hunting and fishing destinations in the country. Trips from 5 cities in the US. 16 years of experience in hunting and fishing.

Phone: 850-386-1213 (US)
flavalle@ba.net

KAU-TAPEN LODGE (F)
Tierra del Fuego, Argentina
Sea-Run Brown Trout

The best stream fishing in the world for trophy sea-run brown trout on the legendary Rio Grande, holding big browns up to 25 pounds. Great accommodations at Kau-Tapen, the southernmost fishing lodge on earth.

Phone: 800-245-1950
www.frontierstrvl.com

LOS CORITOS ESTANCIA (H)
Cordoba, Argentina
Dove

Located approximately 1 hour from Cordoba, Argentina, Los Coritos provides uniformly excellent results—on a typical day, hunters fire from 1000 to 2000 shotshells! The marvelous 8-bedroom lodge/estancia offers all of the uniqueness and charm of a private country manor, but with the convenience of a small, European-style hotel. 4-night/8-shoot Package: $1980 per shooter ($495 per night). Air travel, shells and tips not included.

Phone: 800-211-4753
www.rodgunresources.com

RANCHO SALVAJE DOVE HUNTING (H)
Cordoba, Argentina
Dove

Do you want to hunt where the doves are? We at Rancho Salvaje scout the province each week to find the exact location of grain harvest. What does this mean for you? Less hunting time wasted each day on bad roads. And, because we have many leases with surrounding hotels and ranches, your hunting party is always guaranteed to be where the action is.

Let us do the legwork so you can enjoy your time dove hunting. 4 days: $2100 per person, includes 2000 shells ($800 value) plus airfare, gun permit and tips. Goose hunts also available.

US Agent Phone: 800-422-1321
Fax: 54-11-4713-5528
ranchosalvaje@ciudad.com.ar

RIVER PLATE WINGSHOOTING (H)
Entre Rios Province, Argentina
Duck/Dove/Pigeon/Partridge

There is no region of Argentina that offers a better opportunity for the trip of a lifetime than southern Entre Rios province (north of Buenos Aires). Here a sportsman can experience Argentina's legendary world-class duck hunting, true high-volume dove hunting, and classic partridge shooting over fine pointing dogs. Hunters stay in appealing (sometimes opulent) country homes with names like San Ambrosio, Patria Chica and La Malva, steeped in Old World charm and offering a feeling of genuine hospitality. 4-night/8-shoot Package: $3340 per shooter ($835 per night). Air travel, shells and tips not included.

Phone: 800-211-4753
www.rodgunresources.com

BELIZE

BELIZE FISHING ADVENTURES (F)
Turneff Islands & Belize's Coastal Flats
Tarpon/Permit/Bonefish/Snook

Use the comfort of an air-conditioned mother ship to access all the waters of Belize. Experienced crew and guides make this an exciting fishing adventure for your family or a small group of dedicated fishermen. A very detached, personal, tropical experience with you in control. You and your captain plan the places you'll fish and species you'll pursue. A large resident population of 60- to 100+-pound tarpon as well as baby tarpon are available year-round, along with the greatest population of permit to be found anywhere. Parties of 2, 3 or 4 with an inclusive charter price of $5200 to $8600 for 7 nights. Groups of 5 or 6 are possible.

Phone: 888-347-4896
www.flyfishbelize.com

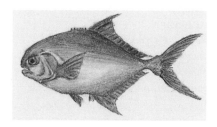

BELIZE RIVER LODGE (F)
Belize
Saltwater Sportfishing

Do you like to fish for a variety of species and in diverse fishing areas? Or do you like to specialize in the grand slam fish? The Belize River Lodge has it all . . . variety of fish species: permit, bonefish, tarpon, snook, cubera snapper, jack crevalle, barracuda, grouper, and diverse fishing areas: flats, cayes, barrier reef, mangroves, channels, Belize River, Sibun River, Manatee River and Black Creek. However, the Lodge specializes in sightfishing our many saltwater flats. We offer a 52-foot Chris Craft, the Blue Yonder, for mother-ship fishing and snorkeling cruises. We also offer spectacular eco tours for the adventurous traveler. Combination fishing and eco tour packages are easily available for the angler or family traveling together. Sample 6N/5D Fishing Package: US $2,145 per person, double occupancy, including round-trip airport transfers in Belize; meeting and checkout services; accommodations; air-conditioning; all meals, including a box lunch, soda and bottled water, guided fishing; daily housekeeping; skiff and fuel; and hotel, and sales local taxes. Not included: airfare to and from Belize, fishing equipment and tackle, alcoholic beverages, tips to guides and staff, Belize departure tax and airport security fees. Same 6N/5D Package: US $1885 per person, based on 4 people to charter.

Toll free: 888-275-4843
bzelodge@btl.net
www.belizeriverlodge.com

EL PESCADOR (F)
Ambergris Caye, Belize
Tarpon/Permit/Bonefish

Located on Ambergris Caye, El Pescador offers some of the best saltwater flats fishing anywhere. Tarpon, Permit and Bonefish are our main focus, but we do offer exciting trips to the reef for other species as well. A perfect location to bring your nonangling companion, as the accommodations are located on a private beach overlooking the world's second-largestbarrier reef. The lodge has a freshwater pool as well as air-conditioned rooms available. Please contact us for references or visit our website PO Box 17, San Pedro, A/C, Belize.

Phone: 011-501-26-2398
www.elpescador.com

M/V CRISTINA (F)
Belize
Saltwater Sporfishing

Belize River Lodge is proud to be the pioneers in mother-ship cruises in Belize. Our newest acquisition is a 58-foot Hatteras, the Cristina. Fishing from a mother ship is the most successful and versatile way to fish the waters of Belize for permit, bonefish, tarpon, snook, barracuda, jack crevalle, snapper and many other species. Mother-ship cruises not only allow for great fishing but also enable easy access to snorkeling and exploring the reef, cayes, beaches and shore areas. Each mother ship comes with its own crew of captain, mate and chef. The Cristina has a master stateroom with a queen bed, which is able to convert to two singles, and a guest room with two single beds; each room has a private bath, with hot and cold fresh water. There are private crew quarters. Sample 6N/5D Fishing Package: US $3145.45 per person, based on 4 people to charter.

Toll free: 888-275-4843
bzelodge@btl.net
www.belizeriverlodge.com

BRAZIL

AMAZON PEACOCK BASS SAFARI (F)
Brazil
Peacock Bass

With River Plate Anglers you will travel about 1 hour from Manaus,

Brazil, via Cessna Caravan floatplane into virgin waters where large populations of giant peacocks remain unmolested. It is common for guests to catch 20–40 peacocks per day with many 8 to 10 pounds, up to 26 pounds. Of course, there is always a chance for a real monster. Anglers enjoy *not* roughing it in either a unique, upscale mobile camp or a 76-foot, fully air-conditioned riverboat. 7N/6D Fishing Package: $3250 per person, cabin barges; $3550 per person, Amazon Angel. Prices based on double occupancy. Air travel and tips not included.

Phone: 800-211-4753
www.rodgunresources.com

AMAZON TOURS (F)
Coppell, Texas
Peacock Bass

Brazil's premier Peacock Bass fishing. 27-lb. IFGA all-tackle world-record Peacock Bass caught with us in 1994, and 500 Peacock Bass over 20 lbs. caught by our anglers last season. The finest land and mobile accommo-

dations are available at either our luxurious Rio Negro Lodge or the famous 85-foot Amazon Queen riverboat. Now offering remote fly outs to private land-locked lagoons. 6 Days of Fishing Package: $4950, which includes airfare from Miami to Manaus.

Phone: 888-235-3874
USA@peacockbassfishing.com

CHILE

SWEENEY'S OUTDOOR ADVENTURES (F)
Chilean Andes and Fjords
Trophy Browns/Trophy Rainbows/ Coho Salmon

From the traditional Chilean fishing lodges in the Andes to the newly discovered rainbow and salmon fishery in Chile's fjords, there are great fishing experiences available. The Southern Hemisphere is a wonderful place to be when the cold gray skies of winter cover the US. We know the great lodges of Chile, including the established outfitters who have explored

the fjords. Mother-ship trips, lodges and even a luxurious hotel/spa—there are many possibilities to experience the best fishing Chile has to offer.

Phone: 888-347-4896

COSTA RICA

CASA MAR LODGE (F)
Barra Colorado, Costa Rica
Tarpon/Snook

Casa Mar Lodge is located away from the local village in its own private 7 acres of tropical garden, a scenic, serene setting. The cabins have two twin beds with private bathrooms and showers. Food is home-cooking style and you'll have all you can eat at every meal. Casa Mar Lodge offers 18-foot custom-built flat-bottom boats providing stable casting platforms and unlimited access into numerous lagoons for smaller gamefish on top water poppers. Guides are English-speaking and knowledgeable in both conventional fishing and fly fishing. All packages include accommodations, ground transportation, all meals, soft drinks/beer and unlimited open bar while at the lodge, fully guided fishing and laundry service. 3N/3D Package, 5N/5D Package, and 7N/7D Package available. Also daily rates that include a one-night stay.

Phone: 800-543-0282
Fax: 714-525-5783

COSTA RICA'S JUNGLE TARPON LODGE (F)
Parismina, Costa Rica
Tarpon/Snook

Costa Rica is all you've heard—economically stable, politically democratic and home to an amazing variety of plants, animals and sportfishing opportunities. 6 days at our remote jungle lodge jumping huge Tarpon and acrobatic Snook, then finishing with 2 days of blue-water fishing on the West Coast targeting Marlin, Sailfish and perhaps Dorado. English-speaking guides, over 100 acres of jungle preserve complete with nesting sea turtles! 6D/5N Package: $1995. 8D/7N multi-coast trip: $2995. Laurence John.

Phone: 800-544-2261
greatalaska@greatalaska.com

CROCODILE BAY LODGE (F)
Osa Peninsula, Costa Rica
Marlin/Sailfish/Roosterfish/Dolphin (Dorado, Mahi)/Tuna/Wahoo/Snook/ Cubera Snapper (Pargo)/Broomtail Grouper

Crocodile Bay Lodge is one of Costa Rica's newest and the most unique resorts in Central America. This first-class resort, adjacent to some of Costa Rica's most beautiful beaches, sits on its own 44 acres of tropical gardens in southwestern Costa Rica (Pacific side) on the Osa Peninsula, which has been described by *National Geographic* as "the most ecologically intense place on earth." 5N/3D Fishing Package: $2195 per person, double occupancy. Includes your first and last night's lodging at a first-class hotel in San Jose; ground transportation between airport and hotel; round trip air between San Jose and the lodge; and all meals including beer, local liquor and soft drinks. Fishing packages also include fishing boats with fuel, tackle, guide and license.

Toll-free: 800-733-1115, 415-209-6177
Fax: 707-778-8077
www.crocodilebay.com

OCOTAL SPORTFISHING RESORT (F)
Guanacaste, Costa Rica
Sailfish/Blue and Black Marlin/ Roosterfish/Dorado/Tuna

Combine the world's most prolific sailfishing with the comfort and amenities of a deluxe beach resort lodge on Costa Rica's north Pacific coast. Catch blue and black marlin year round with exciting seasonal sailfishing. Ocotal is also your best bet in the world for trophy-size roosterfish. Caught year-round, 50-lb. plus roosters are common. Ocotal Resort is a full-service hotel. All rooms have ocean views, A/C, telephone, cable TV, two queen or king beds, room service, etc. Ocotal's fleet of three 32-ft. and one 42-ft. boats are crewed with Costa Rica's most experienced crews. Packages include accommodations, tax, all meals, fishing daily and transportation to and from local airport. 6D/5N Package available with 4 days of fishing. Longer and shorter packages also.

Phone: 011-506-670-0323
Fax: 011-506-670-0083
eloctal@racsa.co.cr
www.ocotalresort.com

RIO PARISMINA LODGE (F)
Parismina River, Costa Rica
Tarpon/Snook

Rio Parismina is a world-class resort lodge located on the Caribbean coast of Costa Rica, built in 1988 on over 50 private acres of lush jungle on the banks of the famous Parismina River. Here you will find superior boats and equipment and many personal comforts, including a pool and Jacuzzi. We offer luxury accommodations, superb food and a wealth of amenities in one of the world's finest Tarpon and Snook sportfishing areas. We offer 3-, 4- and 7-day fishing trips.

Phone: 800-338-5688
fishing@riop.com
www.riop.com

SILVER KING LODGE (F)
Barra Colorado, Costa Rica
Tarpon/Snook

This deluxe sportfishing lodge is situated in the midst of a tropical rain forest where flora and fauna abound. The productivity for tarpon and snook is unparalleled anywhere else in the world. Silver King Lodge offers 24-foot V Hull vessels with 150-hp engines which safely and swiftly get you out to the Caribbean Sea or the many inland waterways. Knowledgeable English-speaking native guides will get you into all of the fishing action that you can handle. The Silver King complex offers large rooms, North American beds, private tiled baths, hot showers, ceiling fans, a hot tub and a large swimming pool.

Delicious meals are served buffet style and the "limited open bar" is always waiting. The fishing season is year-round; however, the summer months of July, August and September are quite wet. The packages include all accommodations, in-country ground and air transfers, guided fishing, taxes and limited open bar.

Phone: 800-231-RICA

HONDURAS

CANNON ISLAND RESORT (F)
Northern Honduras
Royal Tarpon/Snook/Cubera Snapper

Hello! Your friend, Ollie Thompson, thought that you needed a week or so in tropical paradise as far away from the office as possible. Cannon Island is a privately owned island in the remote northern corner of Honduras. We offer fishing expeditions for Royal Tarpon, Snook, Cubera Snapper, and many other big game fish. The only people allowed on the island are our expedition guests like yourself and Ollie Walker and our staff to serve you! When you get a quick moment, check out our new website. We would love to get your comments. If you like what you see, bring Ollie Thompson and come fish with us!

Phone: 503-643-9224
snoviello@gotarponfishing.com
www.gotarponfishing.com

MEXICO

ANGLERS INN/CASA BLANCA LODGE (H&F)
Lake El Salto, Mexico
Bass/Billfish/Duck/Dove

Largemouth bass fishing, light-tackle and offshore saltwater fishing. Fish for trophy bass from our luxury lakeside lodge on world-famous Lake El Salto called the world's best trophy lake by *Bassmaster* magazine. Delicious Mexican and American cuisine. Bass up to 16 lbs. Also, light tackle and offshore saltwater excursions with experienced captains out of Mazatlan. Top-notch Mexican wing shooting on doves and ducks. From November through February, enjoy red-hot wing shooting on the shores of beautiful Lake El Salto. Experience sky-darkening flocks of doves or hunt a wide variety of ducks (including several Mexican species of waterfowl.) Special Cast & Blast packages for hunters/anglers. Stay in luxurious lakeside Casa Blanca Lodge. Owned and operated by Billy Chapman, Jr. U.S. Mailing address: PMB #358, 2626 N. Mesa, El Paso, TX 79902.

Phone: 915-858-8811
info@anglersinn.com
www.anglersinn.com

B&B MEXICO FISHING ADVENTURES (H&F)
Los Mochis, Mexico
Trophy Largemouth Bass

Trophy bass fishing vacations at Mexico's finest bass fisheries—Lake Huites, Lake Agua Milpa, Lake Baccarac and Lake Guerrero. Lake Huites is a great bass fishery where it is not uncommon to catch large numbers of quality bass daily. Lake Agua Milpa is a new up-and-coming lake with great numbers and fish pushing the 13-lb. mark. Lake Baccarac is a well-established bass fishery with great numbers and many bass exceeding the 10-lb. mark. Lake Guerrero is a well-established bass lake which produces large fish on a regular basis. In addition to great bass fishing year round, there is also outstanding seasonal hunting for dove, duck and quail. 4-night/3-day fishing packages start at just $795 per person.

Toll free: 888-479-BASS
Phone: 541-296-3962
Fax: 541-296-9144
www.wheretofish.com

BOCA PAILA LODGE (F)
Yucatan Peninsula, Mexico
Bonefish/Permit/Tarpon/Snook

Species variety is the attribute that best defines the saltwater flats fishing at Boca Paila Lodge. Bonefish, permit, tarpon and snook inhabit an extensive saltwater lagoon system. Beautiful bungalows sit on pristine beach. Excellent food and special hospitality.

Phone: 800-245-1950
www.frontierstrvl.com

CHAPMAN & BALDERRAMA RESORTS, LAKE BACCARAC (F)
Lake Baccarac, Mexico
Largemouth Bass

The fishing lodge is located in the town of Bacubirito, an old gold-mining town in the mountains of Sinaloa state. Lake Baccarac, well known as the best trophy bass lake in the world, holds a record of 19.10 lbs. Bacubirito is best reached by private plane and boasts a paved landing strip of 5200 feet, or you can fly by commercial airline to Los Mochis. Season: October through April.

4N/3D Package: $1195 pp. Includes 3 full days of fishing, guide and boat, meals (lunch served on the lake), soft drinks, beer, margaritas, purified water and group transportation from lodge to lake each day. Air travel, tips and fishing licenses not included.

Phone: 011-52-68-150995
Fax: 011-52-68-120995
Phone: 800-422-1321

CHAPMAN & BALDERRAMA RESORTS, NEW LAKE AGUA MILPA (F)
Tepic, Nayarit, Mexico
Largemouth Bass

Agua Milpa has been acquired by the leaders in bass fishing in the Western Hemisphere with modern rooms and fantastic meals. The lodge is located a 45-min. drive over paved road from Tepic's airport and only 50 yards from the boat dock. Season: October thru June. 4N/3D Package: $1195 pp. Includes 3 full days of fishing, meals, beer and margaritas, boat and guide, filleting and freezing of all fish kept, and ice. Transportation, tips and fishing licenses not included.

Phone: 011-52-32-115128
Fax: 011-52-32-115147

CRAZY FEATHER OUTFITTERS (H)
Tamaulipas, Mexico
Duck/Quail

Enjoy extraordinary classic decoy duck hunting equaled only by Argentina, along with the world's best wild bobwhite quail hunting and sporty mourning dove shooting—all just south of the Texas border in Mexico's state of

Tamaulipas. Outfitter Gerry Glasco provides this world-class gunning with comfortable single-room accommodations, great food and drink, knowledgeable guides and gracious service. 4N/3D Hunting Package: $2800–$3000 per shooter, single occupancy, which includes the use of the lodge's new-model Benelli automatic shotguns (12 and 20 gauge) and hunting license. Air travel, shells and tips not included.

Phone: 800-211-4753
www.rodgunresources.com

DE LA GARZA OUTFITTER'S CASA GRANDE LODGE (H)
Nuevo Leon, Mexico
Dove

Located in a park-like setting near the town of Anahuac in the Mexican state of Nuevo Leon, Casa Grande Lodge accommodates up to 28 discerning sportsmen in true comfort, with excellent food and open bar, service and, of course, the great shooting the De la Garzas are famous for. Personally guided hunts for whitewing and mourning doves are Casa Grande's specialty, and it is probably the only lodge in Mexico whose hunting fields are truly just minutes away—*no long drives*. The lodge itself is easily reached—just a 45-minute drive south of Laredo, Texas. 3-night/5-shoot Package: $1725 per shooter, double occupancy, which includes the use of the lodge's new-model Browning and Benelli automatic shotguns (12 and 20 gauge), tips and hunting license. Air travel and shells not included.

Phone: 800-211-4753
www.rodgunresources.com

EARTH, SEA AND SKY VACATIONS (F)
Cabo San Lucas, Mexico
Marlin/Dorado/Roosterfish/Tuna/ Sea Bass/Grouper/Pompano/Sailfish/ Mackerel/Snapper/Amberjack

Earth, Sea and Sky Vacations specializes in Cabo San Lucas, Mexico. They offer deluxe fishing, golf and dive packages with private villa or beach resort accomodations. Why not let their team of professionals provide you with the personal service you need to make your vacation a dream come true? Come to where the Sea of Cortez meets the Pacific Ocean, and find out why Cabo San Lucas is called the "Marlin Capital of the World." Call toll-free for a free color brochure and video.

Phone: 800-745-2226, 831-475-4800
info@cabovillas.com
www.cabopro.com

FLY FISH THE FLATS (F)
Ascension Bay, Mexico
Bonefish/Permit/Tarpon

Classic trips for bonefish, permit and tarpon fulfill your wildest fly fishing fantasies on the sugar white sand flats of Ascension Bay, Mexico. Located south of Cancun, your Caribbean beach front lodge provides access to endless flats and mangrove islands. Also offshore angling and the incredible beauty of the Sian Kaan Ecological Reserve. All inclusive trips combine all day guided fishing (2 guides/2 anglers per boat) or eco tour, rooms, food and optional side trips for Mayan ruins, bill fishing, diving and Cancun. All fly fish 7D/6N, $2095. Couples Fish & Nature Combo 6D/5N, $1795. Eco Tour 5D/4N, $1495.

Phone: 800-544-2261
Fax: 907-262-8797
Greatalaska@greatalaska.com
www.flyfishtheflats.com

GABINO'S YAQUI VALLEY HUNTING LA ESCONDIDA/ LA NELLITA (H)

Navojoa & Ciudad Obregon, Mexico

Dove/Duck

This world-class combination of classic decoy duck hunting and volume dove shooting centers in the coastal agricultural region of Mexico's two northwestern states, Sonora and Sinaloa. Both whitewing and mourning doves live here year round in abundance (not migrating) and the duck habitat is perfection—endless miles of shallow-water estuaries, mangrove swamp, and freshwater ponds located adjacent to grain and vegetable production. With outfitter Frank Ruiz, at Gabino's Yaqui Valley Hunting you will be in the right place at the right time with delightful accommodations and service, fine food and drink, and—most importantly—abundant game. 4N/3D (2 duck hunts, 4 dove hunts) Package: $2800 per shooter, double occupancy. Air travel, shells and tips not included.

Phone: 800-211-4753
www.rodgunresources.com

HACIENDA LAS PALMAS (H&F)

Lake Guerrero, Mexico

Largemouth Bass/Whitewing Dove/ Bobwhite Quail

Located on the legendary Lake Guerrero in northeastern Mexico, Hacienda Las Palmas offers whitewing dove hunting from mid-August through October, bobwhite quail hunting from November through February and trophy bass fishing year-round. Trips range from $1100 to $2600 for 4 nights and 3 full days of hunting and fishing. Come join us at Hacienda Las Palmas and experience the ultimate sporting adventure.

Phone: 800-285-1803
www.sportsresorts.com

JEFF KLASSEN SPORT FISHING (F)

Los Cabos, Mexico

Marlin/Sailfish/Tuna/Dorado/Wahoo/ Roosterfish/Jack/Pargo

Jeff Klassen Sport Fishing offers sportfishing options in Los Cabos, Mexico. The difference between our operation and that of others is that we utilize the best of the independent boats. In other words, *no* hotel, *no* time share and *no* big fleet boats. Fleet and hotel boats are booked solid by virtue of hotel lobby traffic and travel agents. They generally have the lowest-paid crews and the oldest boats with the oldest and cheapest gear possible to keep them functioning. Independent operators rely 100% on repeat and referral business and know the value of good equipment and friendly, English-speaking crews. Off shore, we target marlin, sailfish, tuna, wahoo and dorado. We also run the very popular surf fishing trips out of Cabo San Lucas during June and July of each year, targeting roosterfish, jacks, snappers and sharks. Contact us for more information.

Phone: 360-402-FISH
Fax: 360-352-6134

info@jeffklassenfishing.com
www.jeffklassenfishing.com

LAGUNA VISTA HUNTING RESORT (H)
San Fernando, Mexico
Duck

Laguna Vista is located on the east coast of Mexico at the convergence of three great North American flyways. Enthusiasts around the world agree that the Laguna Madre of eastern Mexico has some of the best water-fowling anywhere. Our guides are American and highly professional. At Laguna Vista we provide our customers with first-class hotel accommodations. All of our spacious air-conditioned individual rooms have two double beds and a private bath. Our kitchen will prepare steaks, fresh seafood, Mexican food or some of the game that has been brought in. 3D/3N Total Package: $2995 (we provide guns). Some goose hunting available.

Phone: 800-274-4401
carolyngerdes@aol.com

PISCES SPORTFISHING FLEET (F)
Cabo San Lucas, Mexico
Marlin/Sailfish/Swordfish/Tuna/Dolphin/Wahoo

Pisces Sportfishing Fleet has an excellent fleet with a range of vessels to suit everybody's needs, from 28-ft. cruisers to luxury yachts, targeting marlin, sailfish, swordfish, tuna, dolphin and wahoo. Fish the fleet that has the highest return-customer rate in Cabo. The reason: our service. Experienced, friendly guides and first-class service all-around. For fishing charts, photos and more information, visit our web site. Honored by IGFA with the conservation award and also by the Billfish Foundation.

Phone: 011-52 114 31288
Fax: 011-52 114 30588
pisces@piscessportfishing.com
www.piscessportfishing.com

SEACLUSION VILLA (F)
Ascension Bay, Mexico
Permit/Bonefish/Snook/Barracuda

Grand Slam capital of the world. This private villa is located 4 miles from Punta Allen on the Mexican Yucatan. On Ascension Bay, arguably the hottest fishing destination in the world, this hidden villa offers convenient access to a combination of angling challenges. Permit and bonefish are plentiful on the flats, with snook, barracuda and a variety of species to cast for in the lagoons. The most luxurious accommodations you can find on the Yucatan. 7N/6D Fishing Packages available. All-inclusive, with lodging, meals and transfers from Cancun. An Orvis-endorsed lodge.

Phone: 888-829-9420

SINALO PATO DUCK & WING DOVE CLUB (H&F)
Los Mochis, Sinaloa, Mexico
14 Duck Species/Whitewing and Mourning Dove

Mexico's premiere West Coast location for bird hunting. Pintail, Gadwall, Green, Blue and Cinnamon Teal. Black Duck, Canvasback, Widgeon, Redheads, Mexican Tree Duck and others, plus incredible numbers of whitewing and mourning doves, thrive on the marshlands and fertile farming valley of Los Mochis. Attended personally by outfitter/owner Roberto Balderrama, Jr. Deluxe accommodations at the five-star Plaza Inn Hotel, headquarters for the Club and its facilities. Delightful service, fine food and drink, plus abundant game are the norm during the season, October through March. Our packages are all inclusive: 4 nights and 3 days of hunting is $1975 dollars. Saltwater and freshwater fishing also available. Please contact us for more information. Video available.

Phone: 800-862-9026
bookings@sinalopato.com.mx
www.sinalopato.com.mx

URUGUAY

ESTANCIA HASPARREN/ ESTANCIA LA RECONQUISTA (H)
Central Uruguay
Dove/Pigeons/Partridge

Bernardo Barran and Alberto Regusci, Uruguay's foremost gamebird outfitters, blend exceptional mixed-bag gunning with relaxed country living at working estancias. Small parties of discerning sportsmen enjoy this shotgunner's dream, with hunting unsurpassed in South America for its quality and worth. Ably guided with days smoothly organized, you'll hunt partridges over crackerjack pointers; pigeons over decoys; doves on changing terrain—each species in the plenitude of eras past. The estancias, which are located approximately $3\frac{1}{2}$ hours (driving) from Montevideo, Uruguay,

are charming, large and comfortable facilities which accommodate hunters with privacy and luxury. 4-night/8-shoot Package: $2600 per shooter, double occupancy. Air travel, shells and tips not included.

Phone: 800-211-4753
www.rodgunresources.com

OTHER INTERNATIONAL DESTINATIONS

AFRICA

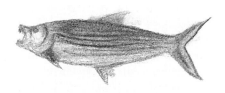

AFRICAN HORIZONS (F)
Durban, South Africa
Tigerfish/Rainbow and Brown Trout/ Kingfish/King and Queen Mackerel/ Bonefish/Sailfish/Bonito/Milkfish/ Bludgers/Springer

Saltwater and freshwater fishing. African Horizons specializes in upmarket, tailor-made fishing, golf, and photographic safaris. All trips are designed from scratch with the clients' personal interests at heart. Come experience brilliant red sunsets from the banks of the mighty Zambezi River, or through the silhouette of a huge acacia tree. See lion, elephant, buffalo, rhino, leopard and a vast array of wildlife and birds coexisting in their natural habitat, mostly undisturbed by human intervention. If fishing is your passion, let us give you the best fresh and salt water fishing on offer. Let us incorporate golf, wine, tribal culture and white sandy beaches with prolific wildlife and exceptional food and drink to create an African adventure that most will only ever dream of. Contact Rob van Blerk.

Phone: 011-27-31-7009833
Fax: 011-27-31-7003397
africanh@iafrica.com
www.africanhorizons.co.za

ASKARI ADVENTURES (H)
South Africa
Trophy Plains Game/Big Five

Specializing in bowhunting. Over 70% of all trophies qualify for SCI medal class. We hunt the areas which provide you with the best hunt (Botswana, Namibia, Zimbabwe, Mozambique and South Africa). Over 40 species of plains game and the Dangerous Seven. Deluxe 3- and 5-Star accommodations and all-inclusive packages. Day rates from $300/day and Bowhunting Safaris from $2995 with trophy fees! Brochure and video available.

Phone: 800-363-4909
www.askariadventures.com

BUSHMEN SAFARIS (H)
South Africa
Plains Game/Big Five

Bushmen Safaris has been an archery only hunting conservancy for 14 years. We hunt one hunt per month, centered around the dark of the moon. The last rifle hunter was in 1986. Bushmen has had an 80% return hunter record for the past 15 years and has taken 98 Top 10 and 219 Top 25 Safari Club International entries. 7-day packages available which include trophy fees. All hunts are customizable. Let us book your African Safari today. Contact our USA office.

Phone: 208-322-5902
www.bushmensafaris.com

OZONDJAHE SAFARIS (H)
Namibia
20 Species of Plains Game

Our 60,000-acre private game reserve is home to an abundance of wildlife. We offer truly first-class accommodations and service, as well as a limited number of safaris, providing our guests with high-quality trophies and an exceptional safari experience. References available upon request. greater kudu, cape eland, sable, roan, waterbuck, gemsbok, hartebeest, blue wildebeest, black wildebeest, impala, springbok, Hartmann's zebra, Burchell's zebra, giraffe, blesbok, steinbok, duiker, klipspringer, damara dikdik, warthog, ostrich, cheetah, leopard, serval, caracal. Wingshooting also available. For information, contact our US office:

Phone: 714-505-4844
jplung@pacbell.net
www.africanhuntingsafaris.com

AUSTRALIA

ERIC BLEWITT SAFARIS (H&F)
Canberra, Australia
Red, Fallow, Rusa and Sambar Deer/ Feral Goat and Ram/Fox/Rabbit/ Brown and Rainbow Trout

Experience hunting and fishing Down Under in the Snowy Mountains region of South Eastern Australia. All hunts are conducted on private land. Fishing for the elusive trout in the southern mountain streams and lakes is offered as an added bonus to clients. Prices for 3 to 5-day deer/goat/ram/night vermin hunts are charged on a daily basis. Trophy fees payable for each species. All prices include professional field guiding, meals, comfortable lodge accommodation and trophy preparation. The perfect vacation for couples and families to enjoy and great opportunity to combine a hunt with other activities including bush walking, snow skiing (in season), horse riding and fishing. Phone Eric Blewitt in Australia.

Phone: 011-61-2-62925434
Fax: 011-61-2-62920090
ericblewittsafaris@bigpond.com

GOVE DIVING & FISHING CHARTERS (F)
Nhulunbuy, Northern Territory, Australia
Marlin/Sailfish/Cobia/Tuna/Mackerel/ Coral Trout/Parrot Fish/Barracuda/ Trevally/Queenfish/Mangrove Jack/ Barramundi/Golden Snapper/Red Throat Emperor

Enjoy 4 to 7-day Guided Wilderness Fishing Safari located in the pristine waters of the Arafura Sea in the Australian Arnhemland "Top End" with over 35 blue-water species to target and some creeks to access mangrove jack, barramundi and other estuary species with professional and locally experienced guides. Very comfortable beachside tent lodge with all meals included and freshly prepared. Islander Adventure 4D/3N Safari: US $1350 incl. GST. Additional cost: Depending on travel route to Gove, anglers may require accommodation in the township of Nhulunbuy the night before and the night after the Safari. Cost for 2 nights, accommodation (1 before and 1 after the safari) US $140 per person, twin share. Single supplement rates are available. PO Box 1630, Nhulunbuy, Northern Territory, 0881, Australia.

info@govefish.com.au
www.govefish.com.au

LONDON LAKES FLY FISHERS LODGE (F)
Tasmania, Australia
Brown Trout

Rated one of the top five fly-fishing destinations by John Randolph, editor of *Fly Fisherman USA*. Large wild brown trout, superb hatches, and Tasmanian wildlife. 5000-acre private estate. Stone and log lodge—10 persons only. Exclusive to fly fishers and their partners. Professional guides. Gourmet meals. "London Lakes is now a valuable addition to my fishing holes. The atmosphere and commitment to excellence in the fishery and every aspect of the lodge are world class and compare with the finest on the planet," wrote Doug Vaday of North Carolina. London Lakes offers unique shallow-water sightfishing. It's "Bonefishing for Trout."

Phone: 011-61-3-6289-1159
Fax: 011-61-3-6289-1122
garrett@londonlakes.com.au

ROCKY CAROSI PROFESSIONAL CHARTERS (F)
St. Helens, Tasmania, Australia
Marlin/Shark/Tuna/Trumpeter/Ling Cod

Professional Charters offers you the choice of 2 first-class sportfishing Charter vessels which will take you to the fishing grounds with speed, safety and comfort. We provide exclusive use of highest-quality Shimano fishing gear, all bait, lures and tackle, morning tea (homemade) and sunblock, with fish cleaned, iced down and bagged. You need to bring sunglasses, hat, camera or video, and deckshoes or soft-soled footwear. Rocky and his crew are dedicated to providing a memorable day of bluewater fishing excitement for both novice and experienced anglers. For group, sole or share charters and any enquiries, contact Rocky and Angela Carosi.

Phone/Fax: 011-61-3-6376-3083
Mobile: 011-61-4-1938-3362
sportfish@vision.net.au

CENTRAL PACIFIC

CAPTAIN COOK HOTEL (F)
Christmas Island, Kiribati
Bonefish

Celebrate Christmas year round at this bonefishing paradise. It's still fresh and unpressured. Weekly departures from Honolulu.

Phone: 800-245-1950
www.frontierstrvl.com

FAR EAST
MONGOLIA (F)
Taimen

Mongolia has one of the planet's largest tracts of untouched wilderness. Spectacular landscape, vast river valleys, huge rolling meadows and, of course, crystal clear rivers full of taimen, lenok and grayling. Where else on earth is it possible to cast dry flies every day to fish over 50 pounds. For most fly fishermen, seeing a 50- to 75-inch taimen explode on a mouse will be the experience of a lifetime!

Phone: 800-245-1950
www.frontierstrvl.com

NEW ZEALAND

CORPORATE SAFARIS (H)
Auckland, New Zealand
Red Deer/Wild Boar/Turkey/Ducks/ Pheasant

Helicopter or 4-wheel-drive transfers from airport to private lodge locations. Individual guides with rifle and ammunition supplied. We can include rainbow and brown trout fishing expeditions on application. Best season is April through August, but year-round for deer and boar. Costs start at US $3950 per person, 6 days/5 nights.

Phone: 011-64-9-535-8570
Fax: 011-64-9-535-8545

alex@fishingnz.co.nz
www.fishingnz.co.nz

FISHING NEW ZEALAND (F)
Auckland, New Zealand
Snapper/Kawhai/Kingfish/Marlin

Each trip individually tailored to budget and fishing preference. Based out of Auckland, New Zealand, your host Alex Carpenter and his wife, Mary, will greet you at Auckland International Airport and return you to their home overlooking the marina and sea to spend your first night recovering from your long flight. Next day, step aboard his Classic 42-foot motor launch and experience the islands of the Hauraki Gulf, fishing and dining on your catch of the day and being entertained with Alex's tales of adventure and good humor. Fish species include snapper, kawhai, kingfish, and marlin in season. Costs: Airport transfers and overnight accommodations US $100 per person. Boat, US $850 per day, including meals and fishing tackle for up to 4 guests. Note: Marlin and game fishing are seasonal and priced separately on application.

Phone: 011-64-9-535-8570
Fax: 011-64-9-535-8545
Mobile: 011-64-2-594-4949
alex@fishingnz.co.nz
www.fishingnz.co.nz

LEITHEN VALLEY TROPHY HUNTS (H)
South Island, New Zealand
Red Stag/Wapiti/Fallow Buck/Tahr/ Arapawa Ram/South Pacific Goat/ Chamois

Hunt our private 5000-acre ranch situated in the beautiful Leithen Valley for red stag, wapiti, fallow buck, Arapawa ram, and South Pacific goat. Fly into the Southern Alps by helicopter to hunt the tahr and chamois. First-class accommodations in our two new lodges, meals, trophy and field preparations, and excellent guides make this an exciting adventure down under.

Phone: 011-64-3-207-2773
Fax: 011-64-3-207-2776
leithen@xtra.co.nz
www.leithenvalley.co.nz

TONGARIRO LODGE (F)
Turangi, New Zealand
Wild Rainbow/Brown Trout

Since 1981 Tongariro Lodge has provided the very best trout fishing and lodging available in New Zealand. Our resident guides are among the most experienced in the country; our clients fish 30 rivers and streams and 5 lakes every season. We run our own rafts, 4WD vehicles, boats and charter helicopter and have some of the best back country nymph and dry fly fishing for sighted browns and rainbows to be found anywhere. Many trophy trout over 10 lbs. are landed each year with an overall average of 4–5 lbs. Room, meals and guided fly fishing based on share twin and share guide: US $355 per day (based on current exchange rate and will vary). For full details look up our website.

Phone: 011-64-7-386-7946
Fax: 011-64-7-386-8860
trout@reap.org.nz
www.tongarirolodge.co.nz or

NORWAY

NORWEGIAN FLYFISHERS CLUB (F)
Norway/Germany
Atlantic Salmon

Fly fishing for Atlantic salmon in Norway offers the chance for the fish of a lifetime. The Norwegian Flyfishers Club leases classic flywater on one of the most productive rivers in Norway, the Gaula River. Easy to reach flying via Oslo to Trondheim. The club has organized a very competent team of guides and the best fishing can be had during the nicest weather periods of the year, from June to August. Fish of 20 to 25 lbs. are common and fish over 40 lbs. can be caught. Hotel accommodations with typical Norwegian food. Packages from $1495 per person. Contact Manfred Raguse, Robert-Blum-Str. 5b, D-22453 Hamburg, Germany.

Phone: 011-49-40-589-2302
Fax: 011-49-40-589-2304
raguse@t-online.de
www.nfc-online.com

RUSSIA

PONOI RIVER CAMP (F)
Kola Peninsula, Russia
Atlantic Salmon

The Ponoi is one of the great Atlantic salmon rivers in the world today. The terrific fishing and stable management is complemented by a superb camp facility and the warm hospitality of a caring Western and Russian staff.

Phone: 800-245-1950
www.frontierstrvl.com

Alphabetical Index to Outfitters, Guides & Lodges

Geographical Index to Outfitters, Guides & Lodges

CARIBBEAN

SOUTH AMERICA & CENTRAL AMERICA

Index to Species

Collins Ranch (New Mexico), 55
Cottonwood Cove Marina (Nevada), 53
Crow Rock Lodge (Ontario), 90
Delta Guide Service (South Carolina), 62
Executive Guide Service (Missouri), 41
Floridian Sports Club (Florida), 28
Four Season Angler Guide Service (Vermont),
71
Gary Martin's Piney Creek Guide Service
(Missouri), 41
Gone Fishin' & Co. (Missouri), 41
Great Plains Guide Service (Nebraska), 53
Hacienda Las Palmas (Mexico), 108
Hampton & Hampton Guide Service (Florida),
29
Hook's Guide Service (Missouri), 42
Iron Mountain Lodge & Resort (Colorado), 23
Just Fishin' Guides (Arkansas), 18
Lake Amistad Marina (Texas), 67
Lake Lanier Houseboat Rentals (Georgia), 31
Lake of the Ozarks Marina (Missouri), 43
Lone Star Guide Service (Texas), 67
Marina at Lake Meredith (Texas), 68
Mark's Guide Service (Texas), 68
Moccasin Point Marina (California), 19
Nickels Farms and Old School Guide Service
(Kansas), 36
Pro Fishing Guide Service (Florida), 30
Rayburn Country Resort (Texas), 69
Roland Martin's Marina & Resort (Florida),
30
Ross' Teal Lake Lodge & Teal Wing Golf Club
(Wisconsin), 73
Rough Creek Lodge Executive Retreat &
Resort (Texas), 69
Running Spring Farm (Missouri), 44
Shirato Outdoor Adventures (Missouri), 45
Slippery Winds Wilderness Resort (Manitoba),
91
State Park Marina (Missouri), 45
Steelwood (Alabama), 1
Sundown Lake Recreational Area (Iowa), 36
Table Rock Lake-Branson Houseboat Rentals
(Missouri), 45
Table Rock Lake Resort (Missouri), 46
Timberline Outfitters (New Mexico), 56
Trinity Lake Resorts (California), 19

Peacock
Amazon Peacock Bass Safari (Brazil), 101
Amazon Tours (Brazil), 101

Fred Mau's Outdoor Adventures (Wyoming),
75
Shirato Outdoor Adventures (Missouri), 45

Smallmouth
Altenhof Inn Bed & Breakfast (Missouri), 40
Beaver Brook Outfitters (New York), 57
Big Cedar Lodge (Missouri), 40
Big Moore's Run Lodge (Pennsylvania), 61
Buster's Guide Service (Missouri), 40
Callville Bay Marina (Nevada), 53
Cottonwood Cove Marina (Nevada), 53
Crow Rock Lodge (Ontario), 90
Dave Spaid Guiding (South Dakota), 63
Eagle Cap Fishing Guides (Oregon), 60
Executive Guide Service (Missouri), 41
Fishing with Jack Wade (Tennessee), 66
Foscoe Fishing Company & Outfitters (North
Carolina), 58
Four Season Anglers Guide Service (Vermont),
71
Gary Martin's Piney Creek Guide Service
(Missouri), 41
Gone Fishin' & Co. (Missouri), 41
Great Plains Guide Service (Nebraska), 53
Hawk Lake Lodge (Ontario), 90
Hook's Guide Service (Missouri), 42
International Angling Adventures (Minnesota),
39
Just Fishin' Guides (Arkansas), 18
La Belle's Birch Point Camp (Ontario), 90
Lake Amistad Marina (Texas), 67
La Reserve Beauchene (Quebec), 93
Manotak Lodge (Ontario), 91
Marina at Lake Meredith (Texas), 68
Moccasin Point Marina (California), 19
New Moon Lodge (Ontario), 91
North Country Canoe Outfitters (Minnesota),
39
Pheasant Crest Lodge (South Dakota), 63
Rodgers Guide Service (North Dakota), 59
Ross' Teal Lake Lodge & Teal Wing Golf Club
(Wisconsin), 73
Shirato Outdoor Adventures (Missouri), 45
Slippery Winds Wilderness Resort (Manitoba),
91
State Park Marina (Missouri), 45
Timberline Outfitters (New Mexico), 56
Timber Trail Lodge (Minnesota), 39
Toe River Lodge (North Carolina), 58
Trinity Lake Resorts (California), 19

Covered Gate Lodge (Texas), 67
Delta Houseboat Rentals (California), 62
Lake Amistad Marina (Texas), 67
Lake Lanier Houseboat Rentals (Georgia), 31
Marina at Lake Meredith (Texas), 68
Rough Creek Lodge Executive Retreat &
Resort (Texas), 69
Running Spring Farm (Missouri), 44
Shangri-La Resort, Conference Center &
Country Club (Oklahoma), 59
State Park Marina (Missouri), 45
Timberline Outfitters (New Mexico), 56

Char

Alagnak Lodge (Alaska), 2
Bearfoot Alaska Resort & Lodge (Alaska), 4
Boardwalk Wilderness Lodge (Alaska), 5
Bristol Bay Lodge (Alaska), 5
Bristol Bay Sportfishing/Iliamna Lake Lodge
(Alaska), 5
Diana Lake Lodge (Quebec), 92
Don Duncan's Alaska Private Guide Service
(Alaska), 5
Fish On! with Gary Kernan (Alaska), 6
4 W Air (Alaska), 6
Fred Mau's Outdoor Adventures (Wyoming),
75
Goodnews River Lodge (Alaska), 7
Great Alaska Fish Camp (Alaska), 7
High Arctic Adventures (Quebec), 92
Holitna River Lodge (Alaska), 8
Inlet View Lodge (Alaska), 8
Katmai Lodge (Alaska), 8
Lake Clark Lodge (Alaska), 9
Midnight Sun Outfitting (Yukon), 96
Mike Cusack's King Salmon Lodge (Alaska),
10
Ouzel Expeditions (Alaska), 10
Rainbow Trout Net (Alaska), 11
Rod & Gun Resources/Alaska Wilderness
Safari (Alaska), 11
Safari Nordik (Quebec), 94
Silver Salmon Creek Lodge (Alaska), 12
Stoney River Lodge (Alaska), 13
Tim's Trophy Lodge (Alaska), 13
White Water Outfitters (Alaska), 15

Cobia

Captain Bo Toepfer's Saltwater Fly Fishing
Guide Service (Maryland), 38

CB's Saltwater Outfitters (Florida), 27
Gove Diving & Fishing Charters (Australia),
112
Offshore Fishing (Florida), 29
Satisfaction Guaranteed Fishing Charters
(Florida), 30
South Seas Resort (Florida), 31
Texas Saltwater Adventures (Texas), 70

Crappie

Barton Ridge Plantation (Alabama), 1
Bear's Den Lodge (Ontario), 90
Buchanan Resort (Tennessee), 66
Buster's Guide Service (Missouri), 40
Callville Bay Marina (Nevada), 53
Collins Ranch (New Mexico), 55
Cottonwood Cove Marina (Nevada), 53
Delta Houseboat Rentals (California), 18
Executive Guide Service (Missouri), 41
Gone Fishin' & Co. (Missouri), 41
Great Plains Guide Service (Nebraska), 53
La Belles Birch Point Camp (Ontario), 90
Lake Amistad Marina (Texas), 67
Lake Lanier Houseboat Rentals (Georgia), 31
Lake of the Ozarks Marina (Missouri), 43
Lone Star Guide Service (Texas), 67
Marina at Lake Meredith (Texas), 68
Moccasin Point Marina (California), 19
New Moon Lodge (Ontario), 91
Nickels Farms and Old School Guide Service
(Kansas), 36
Roland Martin's Marina & Resort (Florida), 30
Ross' Teal Lake Lodge & Teal Wing Golf Club
(Wisconsin), 73
Rough Creek Lodge Executive Retreat &
Resort (Texas), 69
Shangri-La Resort, Conference Center &
Country Club (Oklahoma), 59
Sundown Lake Recreational Area (Iowa), 36
Table Rock Lake-Branson Houseboat Rentals
(Missouri), 45
Table Rock Lake Resort (Missouri), 46
Timberline Outfitters (New Mexico), 56
Trinity Lake Resorts (California), 19

Dolphin

Born Free Charter Service (Bahamas), 97
Charter Boat Kalex (Florida), 27
Fish Rowe Charter Service (Bahamas), 97
Pisces Sportfishing Fleet (Mexico), 109

Walleye

Pompano

Pyrarah

Queenfish

Redfish

Rockfish

Roosterfish

Sailfish

Salmon

Atlantic

Brown

Bull

Sea

BIG GAME

Arapawa Ram

Auodad

Baboon

Bear

Black

Red

Red Stag

Rusa

Sambar

Sitka

Triangle C Ranch (Wyoming), 77
Triple H Hunting (Utah), 70
United States Outfitters, Colorado (Colorado), 25
United States Outfitters, Idaho (Idaho), 34
United States Outfitters, Montana (Montana), 52
United States Outfitters, Utah (Utah), 70
United States Outfitters, Wyoming (Wyoming), 78
Wayback Outdoor Adventures (Alberta), 81
Westwind Guide Service (Alaska), 14
WW Outfitters (Montana), 52

Mountain Goat
Baranof Expeditions (Alaska), 4
Big Timber Guides (Montana), 48
Fred Mau's Outdoor Adventures (Wyoming), 75
Montana High Country Tours (Montana), 50
One Eye Outfit (British Columbia), 83
Parker Guide Service (Alaska), 10
Pioneer Outfitter (Montana), 51
See Alaska with Jim H. Keeline (Alaska), 12
Talisman Hunting Alaska (Alaska), 13
Two Ocean Pass Outfitting (Wyoming), 77
United States Outfitters, Colorado (Colorado), 25
United States Outfitters, Idaho (Idaho), 34
United States Outfitters, Montana (Montana), 52
United States Outfitters, Wyoming (Wyoming), 78
WW Outfitters (Montana), 52

Mountain Lion
Alberta Wild Adventures (Alberta), 79
Bagley Guide Service (Montana), 47
Big Timber Guides (Montana), 48
Blue Creek Outfitters (Colorado), 20
Bugle Mountain Outfitters (Colorado), 21
Circle KBL Outfitters & Guides (Montana), 48
CK Outfitters (New Mexico), 55
Colorado Trophies (Colorado), 22
Cottonwood Ranch Outfitters (Nevada), 54
Cougar Outfitters (Alberta), 80
Darby Mountain Outfitters (Wyoming), 74
Dave Williams Guide Service (Idaho), 32
Double Diamond Outfitters (Wyoming), 75
5 M Outfitters (New Mexico), 55
Flat Iron Outfitting (Montana), 49

Floro Lavalle Outdoors (Argentina), 99
Horizon Guide & Outfitters (New Mexico), 55
Idaho Wilderness Company Hunting & Fishing (Idaho), 33
John McClendon & Sons Guide Service (Arizona), 16
Montana Safaris (Montana), 50
Mustang Outfitters (Nevada), 54
Pioneer Outfitter (Montana), 51
Thunder Mountain Outfitters (Wyoming), 77
Timberline Outfitters (New Mexico), 56
Tom Loder's Panhandle Outfitters (Idaho), 34
Triangle C Ranch (Wyoming), 77
Triple H Hunting (Utah), 70
United States Outfitters, Arizona (Arizona), 17
United States Outfitters, New Mexico (New Mexico), 57
United States Outfitters, Utah (Utah), 70
Wade Lemon Hunting (Utah), 71
World Class Outfitting Adventures (Idaho), 35
WW Outfitters (Montana), 52

Mountain Reedbok
Askari Adventures (South Africa), 111

Nyala
Askari Adventures (South Africa), 111

Oryx
CK Outfitters (New Mexico), 55

Ostrich
Askari Adventures (South Africa), 111
Ozondjahe Safaris (Africa), 111

Rhinoceros
Askari Adventures (South Africa), 111

Roan
Askari Adventures (South Africa), 111
Ozondjahe Safaris (Africa), 111

Sable
Askari Adventures (South Africa), 111
Ozondjahe Safaris (Africa), 111

Scimitar-Horned Oryx
Running M Ranch (Texas), 69

WATERFOWL

Ducks

Geese

MISCELLANEOUS

Rabbit

Varmint

We Value Your Opinion . . .

After visiting any Outfitter, Guide or Lodge listed in this directory, if you will complete and mail in this Evaluation Form you will receive, by return mail, a Certificate good for $10.00 in Bass Pro merchandise. The Certificate is redeemable at any Bass Pro Shops Outdoor World Retail Store, or when ordering through Bass Pro Shops catalogs. It's our way of saying "Thank you" for your help. *Photocopies of this form may be used for multiple visits.*

EVALUATION FORM

NAME AND LOCATION OF OUTFITTER, GUIDE OR LODGE VISITED:

_____

Dates of your Adventure: _____

Were you: Hunting _____ Fishing _____ Both _____

Please rate the following: Excellent   Superior   Fair   Poor

Quality of Facilities   _____   _____   _____   _____
Quality of Meals   _____   _____   _____   _____
Quality of Guides   _____   _____   _____   _____
Quality of Equipment   _____   _____   _____   _____
Quality of Hunting/Fishing   _____   _____   _____   _____
Scenic Beauty   _____   _____   _____   _____

                               Yes   No

Would you return?   _____   _____

Comments:

_____
_____
_____
_____
_____

Your Name: _____

Your Address: (Street) _____
                  (City, State, Zip) _____
                  (Telephone) _____

Please return this completed form to: Marv Fremerman
                                          Outdoor Wilderness Adventures
                                          1955 South Campbell
                                          Springfield, MO 65807